Introduction

When reading the Bible there has always been a question as to why Jesus said that if we call our brother or sister a fool, we are in danger of Hell. In this booklet, I believe we can answer that lingering question.

Life is filled with twists, turns and decisions humans make that affect not only their lives, but also the lives of those in their circle.

In this book, we will discover the difference in the two words translated Hell mention by Jesus Himself, how His words prepare us for the decisions of life, and how they affect us and those we touch with our lives. It is an eye-opening experience as we come to understand the statements made in Matthew 5:21-30. Why is it so wrong to call your brother a fool, and how could lusting after a woman other than your wife cause one to end up in Hell?

I have read the words (as I am sure many of you have) in the Sermon on the Mount and wondered how this could be. I believe that you will celebrate the day that you learned this very eye-opening truth, as I do.

I want you to think on these stories, and when I finish sharing what I believe that God showed me, you will understand the principle of the Gehenna Code.

Sam

Sam became a Christian as a young man. He went to a Christian camp with his youth group, enjoyed the week of camp, and came to realize that he was a sinner and that Jesus came to die for him. He surrendered his life to Jesus and became a born-again believer at that camp. He set his life on a course to do the right thing, going to college to prepare to be a man who could one day take care of the family that he would eventually have. In the process of time, Sam met the love of his life and was on his way to living his dreams. Soon he had a family with a sweet little wife and four beautiful children. Sam was working in a career he enjoyed, but in the midst of his success, something major happened that put him in a bad way. He woke one morning and found himself alone. His family was gone and no one in his family would have anything to do with him; even his own mother and father were giving him the cold shoulder. How on earth did this happen?

What happened was Sam came to a place in his life when he became too busy for God, too busy for family. In turn, he became weak in his faith and convictions, and separated from the precious family that once was his joy. He began to text one of the women at his work and became involved with her. Before he knew it, Sam was up to his eyes in lies and deception. Sam's wife, his kids and even his parents realized that Sam was not the man that he once was. Finally, the truth came out; and now Sam is sitting alone in a world of misery, wondering, "How did I get here, and what do I do now?" The first thing Sam needs to do is to realize where he is. Sam is in the Valley of Gehenna.

Donna

Donna was a young lady who found herself in the middle of a wonderful relationship with the young man of her dreams. Before Donna realized it, she found out that she was pregnant, though the couple was not yet married. She would now have a baby to care for instead of getting ready to go to college like her friends. Even sadder, the "man of her dreams" was not the dreamboat she thought; he now did not want to have anything to do with her. He had his own plans and a baby did not fit into those plans, so he simply abandoned her. What would this young lady do now? Her mom and dad do not know about her situation, and she is facing some big decisions. She is in the Valley of Gehenna! The sad thing is that, no matter what decision she makes, she has created a life that will be forever affected by the decision to go outside of God's design for her.

Tom

Tom was a young man with a wonderful future ahead of him, with scholarships waiting for him to three very large colleges. He was not only planning on going to college, but had hopes of playing pro ball. Tom was going into a world that many can only dream about. Tom had a friend, a young man, who had begun to experiment with drugs. He began with weed and progressed into harder drugs. Tom had always rejected this world, but was suddenly faced with a decision: continue his friendship with this young man, or get away from his influence. Tom did not turn from his friend; he began to go down the road of experiencing drugs. Before Tom realized it, he was sitting in a rehabilitation unit trying to get away from the monster of drug addiction. College scholarships gone and his promising future seemingly fading away, Tom is now in a rehab that should be named Gehenna's Valley. If Tom does not understand where he is and change directions, he just may end up in the local county detention center or even the local mortuary.

Gehenna is a life that is being lived outside of God's will for us. Gehenna comes in many shapes and sizes. The Valley of Gehenna has deep ditches. How far we fall into it depends on how deep we go before we stop or God stops us. God does not want us living in this valley. He will allow us to descend into levels of Gehenna to cause us to call out to Him, but if we are hard of refuse to turn to Him we will just keep digging deeper in Gehenna.

Let us begin!

Outline:

1. Understanding Hades (Hell)
2. Understanding Salvation (the free gift of God)
3. A look at when Gehenna (Hell) came to be a part of the Holy Scriptures.
4. A look at the history of Gehenna
5. Examples of Gehenna in the scriptures
6. The other side of Gehenna
7. Examples of Gehenna in modern times
8. Can a Christian live in the Valley of Gehenna?
9. Do all non-Christians live in Gehenna?
10. What key elements are important to keep us from living in The Valley of Gehanna?
11. How do we move out of the Valley of Gehenna once we discover that we are living there?
12. What did we learn?
13. Conclusion

1. Understanding Hades

The first thing we need to do is understand that there are three words translated Hell in the New Testament. Jesus Himself mentions two of them. There is one more word translated Hell, but is mentioned by Peter in 2 Peter 2:4. Peter explains here that the fallen angels in the days of Noah were placed in a prison cell, waiting for their future judgment. The word he used is "tartaroō." Even the angels suffer the same fate as human creation, as they too either choose to serve God in obedience or to rebel and serve alongside Lucifer (Satan). They will eventually be judged for their rebellion, but now serve as demons, working against God on the planet. Some fallen angels are already jailed in tartaroō, awaiting their future judgement. It seems when reading scripture, angels have three different levels of existence. They work as obedient servants of God, they serve alongside Satan in his rebellion as demons, or are in prison awaiting the final judgment.

But let us talk about the word that most of us think of when we think of the place called Hell, the place where God puts humans who will not submit to His reconciliation. When they rebelled, Adam and Eve were sent out of the Garden, away from God's presence. They did not know it, but they would eventually come to the end of life here, and the place of death would be waiting apart from God. God described the place with one word, Sheol, the Hebrew word used to describe the abode of the dead of the lost. The Greek word for Sheol is Hades, same place but different language.

In Matthew 25:41 Jesus said that the place of everlasting fire was prepared for the devil and his angels. This place was not prepared for humans, but when they rebelled against God, that place away from Him called Hades became the destination of human rebels, just as the rebellious angels. But this is only temporary. The end of the rebellion will take place in the 20th and 21st chapter of Revelation, as God places all those who have rebelled against their Creator and have rejected the rescue payment of Jesus Christ into the lake of fire, calling this, "the second death." This would be the final death, the final separation from God. Angels, and all those made in the image of God who chose to rebel would have the same fate, the lake of fire.

Revelation 20:11-15 *"And I saw a great white throne, and him that sat on it, from whose face the earth and the heaven fled away; and there was found no place for them. And I saw the dead small and great, stand before God; and the books were opened: and another book was open, which is the book of life: and the dead were judged out of those books, according to their works. And the sea gave up the dead which were in it; and death and hell (Hades) delivered up the dead which were in them: and they were judged every man according to their works. And death and hell (Hades) were cast into the lake of fire. This is the second death. And whosoever was not found written in the book of life was cast into the lake of fire."*

All throughout in the Old Testament scriptures, the Bible leaves the afterlife as a pretty big mystery. The reference to eternal separation was either Sheol or the abyss (the pit), and neither one of them was good. Sheol, as we have said, is the place where the rebels went when they died, but the abyss is sometimes translated "the pit." The pit is mainly associated with the bottomless pit in Revelation, which is a symbolic representation of a place of torment and separation from God, but it seemed to be temporary.

The word for pit is mentioned only 11 times in the Bible. The word for Hades is used 10 times in the New Testament; but the Hebrew word for Hades, Sheol, is used 66 times in the Old Testament, all references pointing to the place of separation. Even Jacob made a statement about going to Sheol when he was mourning the apparent death of his son Joseph. When he thought Joseph was dead he was in such depression, he thought that he was going to end up in Sheol. It seems Sheol was a place of terrible punishment; this is what we find when we research Sheol. It is not a good word nor a good end.

The word Gehenna, which we will discuss at length a little later in this material, was used 12 times in the New Testament, and Jesus used it 11 of the 12.

Let us focus on Hades and Sheol.

The first time God mentioned the word Sheol was in Deuteronomy 32:22. From Deuteronomy 32:22 (*"For a fire is kindled in mine anger, and shall burn unto the lowest hell (Sheol), and shall consume the earth with her increase, and set on fire the foundations of the mountains."*) to Jonah 2:2 (*"...I cried by reason of mine affliction unto the LORD, and he heard me; out of the belly of hell (Sheol) cried I,..."*), each mention of Sheol spoke of a separation into a place of sorrow. These 66 times, this word is used to declare a place for the souls of those who did not respond to God as He reached out to them before their soul left their bodies.

As Jesus was speaking to the Jewish people, they knew well the teachings of Sheol. Jesus worked off of this and introduced them to Hades, the Greek word for Sheol, "the abode of the dead of the lost." Jesus began to speak publicly, talking about life and the meaning of life, death and the meaning of death. He began to give us insight into after-death locations and the issues relating to them. In the writings of Luke, he recorded that those who live for the world, when they die, go to a place of torment. We who are in good relationship with God, go to a safe place He calls Abraham's Bosom. This was news! This was news because never had anyone said such things; and He said it with such authority! Let's refresh our memories.

Luke 16:19-31 *"There was a certain rich man, which was clothed in purple and fine linen, and fared sumptuously every day: And there was a certain beggar named Lazarus, which was laid at his gate, full of sores, And desiring to be fed with the crumbs which fell from the rich man's table: moreover the dogs came and licked his sores. And it came to pass, that the beggar died, and was carried by the angels into Abraham's bosom: the rich man also died and was buried; and in hell (Hades) he lift up his eyes, being in torments, and seeth Abraham afar off, and Lazarus in his bosom. And he cried and said, Father Abraham, have mercy on me, and send Lazarus, that he may dip the tip of his finger in water, and cool my tongue; for I am tormented in this flame. But Abraham said, Son, remember that thou in thy lifetime receivedst thy good things, and likewise Lazarus evil things: but now he is comforted, and thou art tormented. And beside all this, between us and you there is a great gulf fixed: so that they which would pass from hence to you cannot; neither can they pass to us, that would come from thence. Then he said, I pray thee therefore, father, that thou wouldest send him to my father's house: For I have five brethren; that he may testify unto them, lest they also come into this place of torment. Abraham saith unto him, They have Moses and the prophets; let them hear them. And he said, Nay, father Abraham: but if one went unto them from the dead, they will repent. And he said unto him, If they hear not Moses and the prophets, neither will they be persuaded, though one rose from the dead."*

This is the declaration that Jesus gave to the world. Hades/Sheol is the place that humans and angels go when they die in sinful rebellion to God. We don't have to make any effort to be in rebellion, because we are born into it (born in original sin). But once we have lived a little while, we prove that we are all sinners and want to be our own boss. Therefore, Hades is not a place that we want to go after we die. Jesus also said in Luke's story that those who die in harmony with

God would go to a place that He called "Abraham's Bosom." We must understand that Jesus is talking to Jews (and the rest of the world, but the audience was primarily Jews), and they had great respect for Father Abraham. They would take comfort in the thought of going to a place of comfort where Abraham was in charge. We have since learned that we now go directly to heaven, to the Lord. Paul instructed the Corinthian church, 2 Corinthians 5:7-8 *"(For we walk by faith, not by sight:) We are confident, I say, and willing rather to be absent from the body, and to be present with the Lord."* The reason for the difference was the cross and the crucifixion. Because Jesus paid the sin debt for the world's rebellion against God and satisfied the judgment on the human race, those who believe the gospel story and trust God for forgiveness will be cleansed form sin; and in that cleansing, the door to heaven will be open to them. This brings new meaning to the words of Jesus as He said "It is finished" as He hung on the cross. He then gave up the ghost, and when this happened the vail in the temple ripped from top to bottom. This provided direct access to the Holy room of God to all who request this forgiveness. Because of this we can now go into God's presence, and as Paul said to the Corinthian Church, to be absent from the body is to be in the presence of the Lord.

In summary, Hades is separation, fire, torment, as Jesus said, and Luke recorded. Other passages declare Hades in the New Testament, but no scripture as clearly as Luke 16. Any serious Bible student knows about the story of the rich man and Lazarus. There is no question that Jesus was declaring the abode of the dead of the lost to be the place that this rich man went after he died, and five times he expressed that he was in torment.

However, when Jesus talked of Hell in His Sermon on the Mount (referenced at the beginning of this book), He did not use the word Hades. There the word Gehenna was introduced to us. While we need to understand the difference (and this is the focus of this writer), let us look at the other places scriptures, where Jesus referenced of Hades first because of it is importance.

Matt. 11:23 *"And thou, Capernaum, which art exalted unto heaven, shalt be brought down to hell (hades): for if the mighty works, which have been done in thee, had been done in Sodom, it would have remained until this day."*

Here Jesus scolds Capernaum for refusing to accept Him and obey His teachings, because Capernaum was the town He lived in for the three years of His ministry. Jesus lived in Capernaum with Simon Peter, Andrew, James and John, as they and their families all lived there. Here Jesus said that this city would be cast into Hades for rejecting Him.

Matt. 16:15-18 *"He* (Jesus) *saith unto them, But whom say ye that I am? And Simon Peter answered and said, Thou art the Christ, the Son of the living God. And Jesus answered and said unto him, Blessed art thou, Simon Barjona: for flesh and blood hath not revealed it unto thee, but my Father which is in heaven. And I say also unto thee, that thou art Peter, and upon this rock I will build my church; and the gates of hell (hades) shall not prevail against it."*

Jesus tells His disciples that when the Church is built, Hell (Hades) "the abode of the dead of the lost," will not be able to win against it. This gives a new meaning to this passage in verse *19 "And I will give unto thee the keys of the kingdom of heaven: and whatsoever thou shalt bind on earth shall be bound in heaven: and whatsoever thou shalt loose on earth shall be loosed in heaven."*

As He finishes this statement, it is clear that He is talking about the world of Hades (death), and the world of Heaven. We have power over both because of who we are in Christ.

In Luke 10:15, Luke records what is said to Capernaum in Matthew 11, and Luke uses the word Hades as well. Luke says that those who do not accept Jesus as the Christ will be cast to Hades at the judgment. It is just that simple.

Acts 2:27, 31 *"Because thou wilt not leave my soul in hell (Hades) neither wilt thou suffer thine Holy One to see corruption." v31 "He seeing this before spake of the resurrection of Christ, that his soul was not left in hell (Hades), neither his flesh did see corruption."* Here Peter was preaching about Jesus after He had been crucified, and he said that God would not leave the soul of Jesus in Hades, neither would He (God) let Him see corruption. Jesus apparently went into the depths of the earth to preach to the fallen angels. 1 Peter 3:18-20 *"For Christ also hath once suffered for sins, the just for the unjust, that he might bring us to God, being put to death in the flesh, but quickened by the Spirit. By which also he went and preached unto the spirits in prison; Which sometime were disobedient, when once the longsuffering of God waited in the days of Noah, while the ark was a preparing, wherein few, that is, eight souls were saved by water."*

Here Jesus went into the depths of Hades to preach to the fallen angels, and Peter was saying that God did not leave Him there long enough to see corruption. While Jesus' body was in the tomb, His Spirit was preaching in Hades to the angels. I know we would like to ask a few questions here, but that is all we have. We don't know much, but one thing we *do* know is that the angels that rebelled were in Hades then and, as far as we know, remain there even now.

Revelation 1:18 *"I am he that liveth and was dead; and behold, I am alive forevermore, Amen; and have the keys to Hell (hades) and death."* Here Jesus declares that He is the one who was dead but lives again and has the keys to Hell (Hades) (the abode of the dead of the lost).

Revelation 6:8 *"And I looked, and behold a pale horse: and his name that sat on him was Death, and Hell (Hades) followed with him. And power was given unto them over the fourth part of the earth, to kill with the sword, and with hunger, and with death, and with the beasts of the earth."* Here the pale horse comes, and his rider has a name, Death, and Hell (Hades) followed behind him.

Revelation 20:13*"And the sea gave up the dead which were in it; and death and hell (hades) delivered up the dead which were in them: and they were judged every man according to their works."* This is the Great White Throne Judgment, and in verse 14 death and Hades are cast into the lake of fire. God has used these to judge those who reject Him, and now He is finished with the judgement of the rebellious; therefore, he throws them in the lake of fire.

Hades is a important word, and understanding it is very important. Understanding eternity is vital for all of God's creation. It is clear that Jesus gave us the teaching of Hades; and every time He talked about the lost after death, Hades was their destination.

It is clear; God will not allow rebellion in His world of blessed eternity (Heaven). The last words of the Bible, Revelation 22:14-21, tell the story. *"Blessed are they that do his commandments, that they may have right to the tree of life, and may enter in through the gates into the city. For without are dogs, and sorcerers, and whoremongers, and murderers, and idolaters, and whosoever loveth and maketh a lie. I Jesus have sent mine angel to testify unto you these things in the churches, I am the root and the offspring of David, and the bright and morning star. And the Spirit and the bride say, Come. And let him that heareth say, Come. And let him that is athirst come. And whosoever will, let him take the water of life freely. For I testify unto every man that heareth the words of the prophecy of this book, If any man shall add unto these things, God shall add unto him the plagues that are written in this book: And if any man shall take away from the words of the book of this prophecy, God shall take away his part out of the book of life, and out of the holy city, and from the things which are written in this book. He which testifieth these things saith, Surely I come quickly, Amen. Even so, come, Lord Jesus. The grace of our Lord Jesus Christ be with you all. Amen"*

God is not going to allow rebellion in His city, His country, His world! Therefore, He sends all rebels to a place He has prepared for rebels. That is the declaration of the book called the Holy Bible.

Before we tackle the word Gehenna, let's get a clear understanding of salvation, and then we will talk about Gehenna. Understanding God's salvation offered to man, how it comes to us, and the power of its promises is key to understanding the difference between Hades and Gehenna.

2. Understanding Salvation (the free gift from God)

Ephesians 2:8-9 *"For by grace are ye saved through faith; and that not of yourselves: it is the gift of God: Not of works, lest any man should boast."*

The word for salvation given to us in the scriptures is a word that was introduced in Genesis (and especially Exodus) as God is delivering His people Israel from hard bondage under the Egyptians. God gives us the greatest picture at the crossing of the Red Sea. Exodus 14:13 *"And Moses said unto the people, Fear ye not, stand still and see the salvation of the LORD, which he will show to you to day: for the*

Egyptians whom ye have seen to day, ye shall see them again no more for ever."

The word for salvation here is the Hebrew word for Jesus. Salvation here is the word listed in the Strong's Concordance number H3444 – Yeshua. The crossing of the Red Sea was God's pictured salvation. He was taking us from Egypt to the Promised Land. In turn, they were miraculously crossing the Red Sea (color no accident) to the next phase of life and into a walk to the Promised Land. Salvation is a lifestyle that is walking with God as His people to the land of promise. Salvation has a beginning and goes on from there, but note: salvation is of God. He created the way; we simply accept and follow.

We quote these verses from Ephesians and trust them, but many people do not realize the comfort in them. These verses declare that salvation cannot be purchased by man. Salvation is given as a gift from God. If we have this salvation, it is because God has offered it to any who will ask the Father for it. Salvation is a gift and cannot be produced or earned by man. This is very important as we go forth.

When Adam and Eve rejected the lordship of God, choosing to make their own decisions in life, God responded by putting them out of the paradise of the Garden of Eden. They began to experience thorns, sickness, pain, wild animals, and even death. I am sure the angels looking on wondered how God was going to find a way to fix the mess man had made for himself and the children to follow.

Here we are getting a glimpse of how God responds to His creation when they go outside of His commands. God has wonderful love for His creation, and wants His creation to live in a way that will be happy and blessed. However, when mankind rebels against God's structure for them, God sets them apart from the blessings that were available to them. As a result of their rejection they find that they are lost.

When God gives us a look at the rebellion in Eden, He also gives us a look at His response. This shows the Gehenna principle that we will discuss in this material.

But how did God begin to declare the answer? We begin to see His approach to this as He killed an animal and made coverings for Adam and Eve. Then we get to chapter 4 of Genesis, where the first two sons of Adam and Eve began a quest to discover a way to get back in harmony with God. Cain went out into the fields and built a great altar and (being a farmer) he cut down lots of his crops and gave God a gift, but God said no. Abel also tried to find the way back to God and Abel went out and he too built an altar, but Abel took a lamb from the field, took the lamb's life, laid it on the altar, and gave it to God … and God said yes.

This made Cain angry. Instead of asking God what he needed to do to get it right, he went out and killed his brother.

When the world reads the story, it is clear that most concentrate on the death of Abel and the drama that comes with this, but that is not the story here. It is *a* story but not *the* story. The question that needs to be asked here is, why did God reject Cain and accept Abel?

There are differing opinions, but I say it was all about the Lamb. Cain gave what he had grown. Even though God had to cause it to grow, Cain plowed the field, Cain sowed the field and Cain watered the field. It was Cain's effort that was offered to God. But Abel gave the lamb. The lamb did the work. Abel built the altar but the lamb gave its life. Abel trusted that God would be happy with his worship if he trusted on the work of another, the work of the lamb!

Salvation is all about trusting what Jesus, God's Lamb, has done for us. John the Baptist said, "Behold the Lamb of God that taketh away the sins of the world". We are saved, we have salvation when we trust the work of Jesus, the Christ.

I have discovered that there are only two religions in the world, but only one will attain salvation. All the religions in the world except biblical Christianity are trying to get back to God as Cain tried, with their own work. Praying, giving, going, doing: all these things are the way of Cain. But the way of Abel is to trust the finished work of the Lamb, a picture of the coming Lord Jesus Christ and His sacrifice for the sins of mankind.

Jesus said to His disciples in Luke 18:31-34 *"...Behold, we go up to Jerusalem, and all things that are written by the prophets concerning the Son of man shall be accomplished. For he shall be delivered unto the Gentiles, and shall be mocked, and spitefully entreated, and spitted on: and they shall scourge him, and put him to death: and the third day he shall rise again. And they understood none of these things: and this saying was hid from them, neither knew they the things which were spoken."*

Jesus said, *"Now is the judgment of this world: now shall the prince of this world be cast out. And I, if I be lifted up from the earth, will draw all men unto me,"* John 12:31-32. Jesus is the life source for our salvation. John 12:44-46 states *"...He that believeth on me, believeth not on me, but on him that sent me. And he that seeth me seeth him that sent me. I am come a light into the world, that whosoever believeth on me should not abide in darkness."*

In Acts 16, we are told that the Apostle Paul and Silas were beaten and thrown into jail. As they worshiped there, God opened the prison doors, but no one left. The jailer, seeing what had happened was moved to ask, *"What must I do to be saved?"* They said, *"Believe on the Lord Jesus Christ and thou shalt be saved..."* We are saved by believing; God is pleased with us because we believe that Jesus is our Lamb. Just like Abel, we trust in the work of the Lamb of God.

Therefore, we are to understand that every person, every group that is trusting in something that they can do to be saved, is doing like Cain, but the ones who are believing in the finished work of Jesus have eternal life; they are trusting like Able.

Now let's talk about eternal life. Eternal life or everlasting life is just that, eternal and everlasting. Understand that the Bible says when I get life from Jesus by trusting on what He (Jesus) has done for me, no one can take it from me. I did not do anything to get it but believe, and I cannot do anything to lose it (or it would not be eternal or everlasting). Think on that just a minute. Eternal life, when one gets it, is just that, eternal – it would not be so if it could be lost.

Therefore, when I read in Matthew 5:22, 29 and 30 that if I do not treat my brother right or if I look at a woman with wrong thoughts I will be cast into Hell (Hades), and I understood that to mean eternal death and hell, I had trouble understanding. You see, the word of God is always in harmony. God's word is consistent. God is not going to tell me in many areas that if I believe on the Lamb and what He did for me I would have eternal life, and then elsewhere that if I said the wrong thing to my brother or looked at a woman wrong I would go to Hell. There is a problem with that thinking, so I knew that there had to be something else here. This is why I kept looking into these passages. There had to be something wrong with my understanding. When I began to do word studies it became clear to me that Jesus was not saying that if I did say the wrong things to my brother or looked at a woman wrong, I was going to Hades (the abode of the dead of the lost). He said that I would be in danger of Gehenna (the trash dump in Jerusalem). This is a big difference! Then I began to research other areas where the words were used differently. What a discovery!

Just as God put Adam and Eve outside the Garden of Eden paradise and into a world of bugs, snakes, wasps, disease, cancer, death, etc., Jesus said that if we did not live in harmony with His will and His words, we would be in danger of living our lives in a valley of stink and death and trash. We are already in the world of disease and death, but there is a world of death within this world of death, Gehenna.

In summary, salvation is a gift and God is not going to take it back if we sin (or He would be doing so constantly, because no one lives perfectly before God either before salvation or after). It is also important to emphasize that, if He took it back, it would not be eternal. Eph. 2:8-9 *"For by grace are ye saved through faith; and that not of yourselves: it is the gift of God: not of works, lest any man should boast."*

3. A look at when Gehenna (Hell) came to be a part of the scriptures

When Jesus preached His Sermon on the Mount, recorded in Matthew's gospel, Jesus was introducing His kingdom principles. The biblical declarations in the prophets' writings (especially the prophet Daniel) declared the coming of God's Kingdom. Daniel gives us the understanding that, when this Kingdom comes, it will grow to the point of taking over the whole earth, and that this kingdom will never end, (Daniel 2:1-44). As Jesus began to introduce His Kingdom principles, He was introducing the eternal Kingdom that He would bring. In the portion of Matthew 6 known as The Lord's Prayer, Jesus told us that we are to pray for this kingdom to come and to bring the will and the actions of the heavenly kingdom down to earth. Matt. 6:7-10 *"...when ye pray, use not vain repetitions, as the heathen do: for they think that they shall be heard for their much speaking. Be not ye therefore like unto them: for your father knoweth what things ye have need of, before ye ask him. After this manner therefore pray ye: Our Father which are in heaven, Hallowed be thy name. Thy kingdom come. Thy will be done in earth, as it is in heaven."*

In Matthew 5:3, 10 and 17-20, Jesus declared this Kingdom teaching. The Kingdom of Jesus is coming down to the earth and those who are a part of this kingdom will live by these principles. We sometimes struggle to understand some of the things that Jesus said in preaching these principles. This is one of those statements that seemed confusing, but I believe that we can get a handle on this one (and it is a very important one). Let us grasp these thoughts. If one wants to live in the Kingdom on earth (walking in the ways of God's teachings), the benefits of God's blessings will be his. However, if one does not begin to follow those kingdom teachings now, he has the potential of living in Gehenna now.

As Jesus taught His kingdom principles for this earth, He introduced this word Gehenna into His teaching. Before this teaching, we had no concept of this word. James later used this word to describe a person that has a cruel tongue but other than that, this word was used and explained by Jesus only.

In studying before, I just could not accept Matthew 5:22 – 30 to be what I originally understood, because my way of thinking conflicted with the other words of Jesus and the rest of the Bible. One must understand that the Bible is not at odds with itself. The Old Testament was and is the declaration of the coming of the New Testament. The Old fulfilled in the New! When we read something in the Bible that seems to conflict with the other parts of the Word of

God, we are missing something. The teaching of Gehenna is one of the greatest examples of this.

Saying that, let me ask a question: where do we put things that we discard, things we reject? We put them in the trash! The trash goes to the landfill in America, and we push it into a hole and cover it up. But in Jesus' day, they took it to the valley of Gehenna, where the fires continually burned and the worms continually ate on it. The stink of it was horrible and the sight of it was just as bad.

Every verse that uses the Greek word Hades points to the place where the soul that does not know God through Jesus Christ goes after death. But Jesus introduced us to a whole new word translated Hell, but this is Hell on earth; that word is Gehenna. In Matthew 5, as He pronounced His public Sermon on the Mount, Jesus proclaimed the blessings of being a part of His kingdom.

Matthew 5:3-12 *"Blessed are the poor in spirit: for theirs is the kingdom of heaven. Blessed are they that mourn: for they shall be comforted. Blessed are the meek: for they shall inherit the earth. Blessed are they which do hunger and thirst after righteousness: for they shall be filled. Blessed are the merciful: for they shall obtain mercy. Blessed are the pure in heart: for they shall see God. Blessed are the peacemakers: for they shall be called the children of God. Blessed are they which are persecuted for righteousness sake: for theirs is the kingdom of heaven. Blessed are ye, when men shall revile you, and persecute you, and shall say all manner of evil against you falsely, for my sake. Rejoice and be exceedingly glad: for great is your reward in heaven: for so persecuted they the prophets which were before you."*

In these verses, we are told that we would be blessed on earth and in heaven for walking in the way that the kingdom demands. But as Jesus continued to preach, He began to give the other side of the coin, so to speak, and that was Gehenna. He explained that his followers are salt and light, and they will receive a blessing, when they are a blessing. But He then began to explain what would come to those who disregarded the teachings of the kingdom.

This word Gehenna is used 12 times in the New Testament and Jesus used it 11 of the 12.

Let us look at those uses:

Matthew 5:22, 29, 30: Here in the Sermon on the Mount Jesus is giving Kingdom principles. As He begins the sermon with the words "Blessed are those who...," it is clear that He wants us to understand that His kingdom principles are the way to live. Here in this sermon Jesus introduces "The Gehenna Code," which is what this book is all about. Here Jesus said that if we do not speak to our brothers in a healthy way, we will be in danger of being in Gehenna. If we do not look at other women in a god-honoring way, we will be in danger of Gehnna.

Matthew 10:28: Here in a private meeting, Jesus also explained that it is important to fear God (and fear a life without God) because Gehenna is the alternative to walking with God. Matthew 10:28 *"...fear not them which kill the body, but are not able to kill the soul: but rather fear him which is able to destroy both soul and body in hell (Gehenna).*

Matthew 18:7-9: In this message to His followers, He tells them that if we are offended at others, we are in danger of Gehenna. He says in verse 7 *"Woe unto the world because of offense...,"* Why? Gehenna is waiting on the ones who are offense driven. When we are offended at others and do not forgive them, Gehenna, the trash filled valley, is waiting for us. When we build fences between us and other people, Gehenna is waiting!

I had a friend many years ago who had a problem with offense. He would get offended by everyone, and he continually alienated himself from everyone until he was sitting alone with not even one good friend. This man is a classic example of one who moved into the Valley of Gehenna. Wife gone, children gone, brothers and sisters gone; his grandchildren would not even come to see him. This man is classic Gehenna man. Jesus was telling even His kingdom people that they could be part of His kingdom and still live in Gehenna on earth. Yes, heaven is their eternal home, but Gehenna is their earthly residence.

Matthew 23:15, 33: Here Jesus speaks harshly to the Scribes and the Pharisees. He says that they who are rejecting Him and His teaching are not only children of Gehenna, but when they convert one to follow them, they create a person who is worse than they are in Gehenna. He tells them that because of their approach to Him, they cannot escape the grasp and of the damnation of Gehenna.

Mark 9:43, 45, 47: Here in Mark, it is easy to confuse Gehenna with Hades, because He is talking about being cast into the place of fire and worms, but how do fire and worms exist together (and why fire and worms)? Because He is talking about the trash valley of Jerusalem.

Luke 12:5: *"But I will forewarn you whom ye shall fear: Fear him, which after he hath killed hath power to cast Into hell (Gehenna); yea, I say unto you, Fear him."*

In this passage, Jesus says that we are not to fear the one who has the power to destroy the body; we are to fear the one who has the ability to destroy by throwing both body and soul into Gehenna. We simply assume that it is eternal Hell, but the word Gehenna is the trash valley. It is apparent that Jesus was saying that being cast into the trash valley of Jerusalem would lead to destruction, of the body as well as the soul. When you and I see some of the results of living apart from God's direction, we understand that it is destructive living in the valley of Gehenna (or should I say, dying in Gehenna?).

James 3:6 *"...the tongue is a fire, a world of iniquity, so is the tongue among our members, that it defileth the whole body, and setteth on fire the course of nature; and it is set on fire of **Hell (Gehenna)**."*

Here James says that when we use our tongue (our words) in a destructive fashion, we produce the product of death in the lives of the people in our world. When we make our lives in Gehenna, it is simply a slow and destructive death. This is saying that we have the power in our words to put someone in Gehenna, in turn putting ourselves in Gehenna, the trash place of life.

Let us discover what Jesus said and why this writer believes why He said it?

4. A look at the history of Gehenna

When Jesus introduced this Greek word, Gehenna, the people listening to him had a history with this area already, but it was called the Valley of the son of Hinnom. The Valley of the son of Hinnom was where the Canannites worshipped the heathen god Molech and sacrificed babies in the fire to him. It was also called the Valley of the Slaughter for that reason. Jeremiah referred to this valley in Chapters 7 and Chapter 19 of Jeremiah. In Jeremiah 32, he calls this valley an abomination as he is referring to the children that were killed here in sacrifice to Molech, even by the Israelites, during the rule of Manasseh.

Jeremiah 7:30-32 *"For the children of Judah have done evil in my sight, saith the LORD: they have set their abomination in the house* which is called by my name, to pollute it. And they have built the high places of Tophet, which is in **the valley of the son of Hinnom**, to burn their sons and their daughters in the fire; which I commanded them not, neither came it into my heart. Therefore, behold, the days come, saith the LORD, that it shall no more be called Tophet, nor the valley of the son of Hinnom, but **the valley of the slaughter**: for they shall bury in Tophet, till there be no place."

Jeremiah 19:2-6: "And go forth unto the valley of the son of Hinnom, which is by the entry of the east gate, and proclaim there the words that I shall tell thee, And say, Hear ye the word of the LORD, O kings of Judah, and inhabitants of Jerusalem; Thus saith the LORD of hosts, the God of Israel; Behold, I will bring evil upon this place, the which whosoever heareth, his ears shall tingle. Because they have forsaken me, and have estranged this place, and have burned incense in it unto other gods, whom neither they nor their fathers have known, nor the kings of Judah, and have filled this place with the blood of innocents; They have built also the high places of Baal, to burn their sons with fire for burnt offerings unto Baal, which I commanded not, nor spake it, neither came it into my mind. Therefore, behold, the days come, saith the LORD, that this place shall no more be called Tophet, nor the valley of the son of Hinnom, but The **valley of slaughter**."

Jeremiah 32:35 "And they built the high places of Baal, which are in the valley of the son of Hinnom, to cause their sons and their daughters to pass through the fire unto Molech; which I commanded them not, neither came it into my mind, that they should do this abomination, to cause Judah to sin."

2 Chronicles 28:3 and 33:6 the kings were guilty of this rebellion against God. Ahaz and Manasseh, kings of Judah, both burned incense in the valley of the son of Hinnom, and burned children in the fire. **After this abomination the LORD cast them out of the land.**

This valley was also <u>called **the Valley of the Giants**</u>, because the people who inhabited this area before the Israelites conquered and made it their land were very large people, so-called giants. Remember the conversation between Moses and the 12 spies in Numbers 13 as they returned from spying out the land? They said that the land was filled with giants. Apparently, they passed through the area of this valley.

As you can see, this valley had some history with Israel, and it was not good history. Therefore, when Jesus began to mention this valley, it was a big deal and it was not confusing for them; they knew about this valley. We are the ones who have been confused. We simply have the mindset of Hell being the eternal place of lost souls, but that is not what this refers to. I am sure that you will see this as we finish.

Keep in mind that Jeremiah was called the weeping prophet because he knew that God had taken the northern tribes into Assyria. Now he knew that God had used him to warn Judah (the southern kingdom) of the same demise. He knew they would not listen, so they too would be taken away and placed outside of God's favor, into what I believe Jesus called a life in Gehenna (the trash heap of life).

<u>This Gehenna principle</u> is consistent in many characters of the Bible.

5. Examples of Gehenna in the scripture

This word Gehenna was introduced by Jesus in His Sermon on the Mount, but the principle of Gehenna is not new. Let us look together at other places where God displays this Gehenna principle.

The Gehenna Principle is living outside the will of God, outside of harmony with God. When man steps outside of obedience, the moving trucks arrive and we are moved into the Valley of Gehenna (the trash heap).

This teaching may seem strange to you, but Jesus was giving us a simple principle that starts in Eden and goes all the way through the Bible with example after example. This is a principle that cannot be denied. It was there all the time, but Jesus put a name to it; He called this place of disharmony Gehenna! We are going to learn that Gehenna is the trash heap of life. The only question is how deep in the trash one chooses to live. This is determined by just how far into rebellion we choose to be. Let us talk about this principle from the pages of the Word of God.

Adam and Eve were the first examples of this teaching. Adam and Eve was created and placed in paradise, the Garden of Eden. Eden means paradise, and that is where He wanted His creations to live. But when Adam and Eve turned from obeying God and chose to be gods unto themselves, they were removed from paradise and placed outside Eden in a world of disease, destruction and death. This was much more than a step down. It took a while before they realized just how bad this new address would be. The principle is the same as Gehenna. Jesus was trying to get His followers to understand that if they did not live in accordance with His word and His will, they would live in a world of death, destruction and disease, He simply called it Gehenna. However, we learn that this was only the beginning. Gehenna could be simple briars and this world's destructive interactions with animals, briars, and death. But it would even be worse depending on how far we choose to go away from God's design for us.

Cain chose to rebel instead of submitting to God. He then killed his brother instead of repenting and complying, and spent his life in hell on earth, Gehenna. Like Adam and Eve, he was sent away and lived in a land where he had the mark of rebellion on him. He did not die until God said that he could, but he lived in a type of hell on earth for the rest of his life, and in turn brought his family into the hell that he had created for himself.

Those who rebel against God not only are alienated from God into a second rate life; they raise their children in that Gehenna on earth. They have the whole world to choose where they will live but they choose rebellion, with the address:

> Cain, Son of Adam
> 6 Rebellion Rd.
> Gehenna, Earth 66666

Notice what the New Testament writer, Jude, said about Cain and a few other rebellious leaders' Gehenna residence.

Jude 1:11-13 *"Woe unto them! for they have gone in the way of Cain, and ran greedily after the error of Balaam for reward, and perished in the gainsaying Core. These are spots in your feasts of charity, when they feast with you, feeding themselves without fear: clouds they are without water, carried about of winds; trees whose fruit withereth, without fruit, twice dead, plucked up by the roots; Raging waves of the sea, foaming out their own shame; wandering stars, to whom is reserved the blackness of darkness for ever."*

We have mentioned Cain, but who is Balaam? In Numbers 22, God tells us about a prophet who is asked by Balak, the king of the Moabites, an enemy of Israel, to curse Israel. Balaam told the king he could not do so unless God gave him permission, and God told him no. However, Balaam continued to come to God and request permission to curse Israel, because the Moabites were offering him a lot of wealth to do so. After many times telling Balaam no, He finally told Balaam to accompany the king's men. However, when he tried to go, God placed a large angel in the road to block his way. Balaam did not even see this angel, but the donkey that he was riding saw the angel and would not try to go past. Balaam became angry and beat the donkey. God gave the donkey the ability to talk and tell Balaam about the angel. As you can imagine, the prophet Balaam lost his prophetic influence with God and man and spent the rest of his life as a by-word and an example of what a man of God is **not** to do. He lived the rest of his life as a disgrace. Yes, even a prophet of God can move to Gehenna.

>Balaam Prophet of God
>6 Rebellion Avenue
>Gehenna Earth 66666

Korah was also a by-word for the Jews. The Israelites knew of his rebellion in the days of Moses, and how God opened up the earth and destroyed him and all who partnered with him to rebel against Moses, God's anointed servant.

King Saul was also one tremendous example of how God's favor was lost as a result of rebellion as to what God had or had not said. King Saul not only died a miserable death, but he also lived a miserable life, a life in what could be called "the Valley of Gehenna." God had given him every opportunity to be great and to enjoy the good graces of God, but instead of living in the graces of God, King Saul lived in depression and oppression and even died by falling on his own sword.

This story is listed in 1 Samuel from chapter 9 through chapter 31. When you read the story of his life, you will find that Saul was chosen to be the King of Israel, even though it was not God's desire to give them a king. He gave them a king because they were determined they wanted one. King Saul started pretty well, but he received the will of God for his life and his kingdom from the prophet of God. Samuel was the mediator between King Saul and God.

Saul's first act of rebellion came as he was leading a battle against the Philistines in 1 Samuel 13. Saul was waiting for the priest to come and give the sacrifice before the battle began, and the priest was late getting there. Saul became scared that the enemy would attack before the sacrifice was made so he (King Saul) made the sacrifice himself. Then Samuel came on the scene and confronted him, telling him God was not pleased that he had stepped out of faith in God in fear and made a sacrifice only the priest should have made. That was the first act of rebellion.

The second is recorded in 1 Samuel 15. Saul was given instruction to kill all his enemies during a specific battle, but instead of doing what God had said, he gathered the sheep (and even the king to give to God). Samuel killed the enemy king himself, and told Saul that his rebellion had lost him the kingdom. It wasn't long before David was anointed as king. Even though Saul was living in the palace of the king, he really lived at:

> King Saul, Son of Kish
> 6 Rebellion Street
> Gehenna Israel 666

David and his family—King David is one of the most beloved Bible characters. David appears in the late half of 1 Samuel, and takes up a big part of 2 Samuel. David was the anointed shepherd who became king and, without question, won the heart of God. However, selfishness leads to sin and sin leads to separation; and David, in a selfish time, committed a terrible act of iniquity. God set him aside in misery and what I would call "the Land of Gehenna." David, after his sin, was still the king and was still David, but these acts of sin had robbed him of the precious closeness to his God. We read of his misery and confession in Psalms 51, as David pleaded to move from Gehenna back to the palace (figuratively).

Psalms 51: *"...Have mercy upon me, O God, according to thy lovingkindness: according unto the multitude of thy tender mercies blot out my transgressions. Wash me thoroughly from mine iniquity, and cleanse me from my sin. For I acknowledge my transgressions: and my sin is ever before me. Against thee, thee only, have I sinned and done this evil in thy sight: that thou mightiest be justified when thou speakest, and be clear when thou judgest. Behold, I was shapen in iniquity; and in sin did my mother conceive me. Behold, thou desirest truth in the inward parts: and in the hidden part thou shalt make me to know wisdom. Purge me with hyssop and I shall be clean: wash me, and I shall be whiter than snow. Make me to hear joy and gladness; that the bones which thou hast broken may rejoice. Hide thy face from my sins, and blot out all mine iniquities. Create in me a clean heart, O God; and renew a right spirit within me. Cast me not away from thy presence; and take not thy Holy Spirit from me. Restore unto me the joy of thy salvation; and uphold me with thy free spirit. Then will I teach transgressors thy ways; and sinners shall be converted unto thee. Deliver me from blood-guiltiness, O God, thou God of my salvation: and my tongue shall sing aloud of thy righteousness. O Lord, open thou my lips; and my mouth shall show forth thy praise. For thou desirest not sacrifice; else would I give it: thou delightest not in burnt offering. The sacrifices of God are a broken spirit: a broken and a contrite heart, O God, thou wilt not despise. Do good in thy good pleasure unto Zion: build thou the walls of Jerusalem. Then shalt thou be pleased with the sacrifices of righteousness, with burnt offering and whole burnt offering: then shall they offer bullocks upon thine altar."*

I wanted you to have access to read this man's prayer. David was once walking in the grace of God, and God was pleased to empower and bless everything David did. However, after David rebelled and chose to disobey God, even he found himself in a world of sorrow and despair. Gehenna on earth!

You can find the story of David's rebellion in 1 Samuel 11, the prophet Nathan confronting him over his sin in 1 Samuel 12, and the rest of David's misery in the rest of 2 Samuel. David had one child die after Bethsheba gave birth. One of his sons raped his own half-sister, and one of his sons killed the brother that did the attacking and then died after rebelling against his dad. David cried in deep despair knowing that he was the one who brought his family into this destruction. David's world went from dwelling in the grace and prosperity of God to the Valley of Gehenna, all in one decision. And yes, this one decision drove David to make many more decisions and in the process alienated David from the harmony and blessings of God. Notice, David did not just take himself out of God's gracious blessings; he also took his family with him. David moved his family from the palace of Israel to the valley of Gehenna (figuratively).

Solomon was the son of King David and yes, he was the son of Bethsheba, the child that they had after they lost the first child. Solomon was the last son of King David; therefore, it was a real move of God for him to become King of Israel, since he had many brothers ahead of him. However, God made it so, and we believe that this was a declaration to David by God that he had been forgiven.

Solomon was a wonderful king in his early days, but in his older years he began to allow his many wives to bring worship of other gods into the nation of Israel; and God began to bring a miserable spirit into his heart. Solomon is a good example of a man who had the grace of

God on him as he began his work on earth but his life turned into Gehenna.

Let us examine the difference in this man's life. It is hard to believe that it is the same man.

1 Kings 3:3-14 *"And Solomon loved the LORD, walking in the statutes of David his father: only he sacrificed and burnt incense in high places. And the king went to Gibeon to sacrifice there; for that was the great high place: a thousand bunt offerings did Solomon offer upon that altar. In Gibeon the LORD appeared to Solomon in a dream by night: and God said, Ask what I shall give thee. And Solomon said, Thou hast shewed unto thy servant David my father great mercy, according as he walked before thee in truth, and in righteousness, and in uprightness of heart with thee; and thou hast kept for him this great kindness, that thou hast given him a son to sit on his throne, as it is this day. And now O LORD my God, thou hast made thy servant king instead of David my father: and I am but a little child: I know not how to go out or come in. And thy servant is in the midst of thy people which thou hast chosen, a great people, that cannot be numbered nor counted for multitude. Give therefore thy servant an understanding heart to judge thy people, that I may discern between good and bad: for who is able to judge this thy so great a people? And the speech pleased the LORD, that Solomon had asked this thing. And God said unto him, Because thou hast asked this thing, and hast not asked for thyself long life; neither hast asked riches for thyself, nor hast asked the life of thine enemies; but hast asked for thyself understanding to discern judgment; Behold, I have done according to thy words: lo I have given thee a wise and an understanding heart; so that there was none like thee before thee, neither after thee shall any arise like unto thee. And I have also given thee that which thou hast not asked, both riches, and honour: so that there shall not be any among the kings like unto thee all thy days.*

Then God added this promise as well:

"And if thou wilt walk in my ways, to keep my statutes and my commandments, as thy father David did walk, then I will lengthen thy days."

You and I can read in 1 Kings 3:16 how king Solomon's wisdom was exercised.

In the day of the Kings, a king served as a judge of the people. When there was an issue, the king would render a verdict, just as a judge does today in our world. In 1 Kings 3:16 let us examine the beginning of the wise King Solomon. Vs 16 *"Then came there two women, that were harlots, unto the king, and stood before him. And the one woman said, O my lord, I and this woman dwell in one house; and I was delivered of a child with her in the house. And it came to pass the third day after that I was delivered, that this woman was delivered also: and we were together; there was no stranger with us in the house, save we two in the house. And this woman's child died in the night; because she overlaid it. And she arose at midnight, and took my son from beside me, while thine handmaid slept, and laid it in her bosom, and laid her dead child in my bosom. And when I rose in the morning to give suck, behold it was dead: but when I had considered it in the morning, behold, it was not my son, which I did bear. And the other woman said, Nay; but the living is my son, and the dead is thy son. And this said, No, but the dead is thy son and the living is my son. Thus they spake before the king. Then said the king, The one saith, This is my son that liveth, and thy son is dead: and the other saith, Nay: but thy son is dead, and my son is the living. And the king said, Bring me a sword. And thy brought a sword before the king. And the king said, Divide the living child in two ad give half to the one and half to the other. Then spake the woman whose the living child was unto the king, for her bowls yearned upon her son, and she said, O my lord,* give her the living child, and in no wise slay it. But the other said, Let it be neither nor thine, but divide it. Then the king answered and said, Give her the living child, and in no wise slay it: she is the mother thereof. And all Israel heard of the judgment which the king had judged; and they feared the king: for they saw that the wisdom of God was in him to do judgment."

This was the man to whom God had given His blessing; and it is hard to read of this king and then read the words of Solomon in Ecclesiastes and believe that it is the same man.

But Solomon began to make decisions that were outside of God's instruction, and in turn the land of Israel became a place where false gods were worshiped. The descent into Gehenna followed those decisions, and when Solomon grew older and wrote the book of Ecclesiastes, he penned these words: Ecclesiastes 1:12-18 *"I the Preacher was king over Israel in Jerusalem. And I gave my heart to seek and search out by wisdom concerning all things that are done under heaven: this sore travail hath God given to the sons of man to be exercised therewith. I have seen all the works that are done under the sun; and, behold, all is vanity and vexation of spirit. That which is crooked cannot be made straight: and that which is wanting cannot be numbered. I communed with mine own heart, saying, Lo I am come to great estate, and have gotten more wisdom than all they that have been before me in Jerusalem: yea my heart had great experience of wisdom and knowledge. And I gave my heart to know wisdom, and to know madness and folly: I perceived that this also is vexation of spirit. For in much wisdom is much grief: and he that increaseth knowledge increased sorrow. Chapter 2:1- I said in mine heart, Go to now, I will prove thee with mirth, therefore enjoy pleasure: and behold, this also is vanity."*

The same Solomon who was known for his wisdom became known for his frustration and unhappy life. In this book, I am trying to point out that it is because Solomon turned from humility and gratitude to worldliness and rebellion, contrary to God's instruction. This is a life that I believe Jesus was calling Gehenna!

The man Solomon was also one of the great examples of God's grace being abused; as a result Solomon ended up in Gehenna instead of Eden. As you read on in Ecclesiastes, you see this man of wisdom began to grow more and more frustrated because of the decisions that he made in his life.

Ahab and Jezebel—As for these two, the king and queen of the northern kingdom of Israel, they have always been known for their rebellion and their pointed rejection of God. Even though they were in Israel and were serving as the King and Queen of Israel, they had made a point to reject God's Word (God's way) and in turned lived their lives in what I believe Jesus would call Gehenna. They did not enjoy the blessings of God, nor did they benefit from God's promises; both lived in rebellion and died in rebellion as well. Ahab was supposed to be the King of Israel, but he became the King of Gehenna!

1 Kings 16:29 *"And in the thirty and eighth year of Asa king of Judah began Ahab the son of Omri to reign over Israel: and Ahab the son of Omri reigned over Israel in Samaria twenty and two years. And Ahab the son of Omri did evil in the sight of the LORD above all that were before him. And it came to pass, as if it had been a light thing for him to walk in the sins of Jeroboam the son of Nebat, that he took to wife Jezebel the daughter of Ethbaal king of the Zidonians, and went and served Baal, and worshipped him. And he reared up an altar for Baal in the house of Baal, which he had built in Samaria. And*

Ahab made a grove; and Ahab did more to provoke the LORD God of Israel to anger than all the kings of Israel that were before him."

To put Ahab into context, he and Jezebel, his wife, were ruling when Elijah the prophet prayed for no rain for three years and then called fire out of heaven on Mount Carmel. Both Ahab and Jezebel lived and died in shame and misery.

Manasseh 2 Chronicles 33:1-11 "*Manasseh was twelve years old when he began to reign, and he reigned fifty and five years in Jerusalem: But did that which was evil in the sight of the LORD, like unto the abominations of the heathen, whom the LORD had cast out before the children of Israel. For he built again the high places which Hezekiah his father had broken down, and he reared up altars for Baalim, and made groves, and worshiped all the host of heaven, and served them. Also he built altars in the house of the LORD, whereof the LORD had said, in Jerusalem shall my name be for ever. And he built altars for all the host of heaven in the two courts of the house of the LORD. And he caused his children to pass through the fire in the valley of the son of Hinnom: also he observed times, and used enchantments, and used witchcraft, and dealt with a familiar spirit, and with wizards: he wrought much evil in the sight of the LORD, to provoke him to anger. And he set a carved image, the idol which he had made, in the house of God, of which God had said to David and to Solomon his son, In this house, and in Jerusalem, which I have chosen before all the tribes of Israel, will I put my name forever. Neither will I any more remove the foot of Israel from out of the land which I have appointed for your fathers; so that they will take heed to do all that I have commanded them, according to the whole law and the statutes and ordinances by the hand of Moses. So Manasseh made Judah and the inhabitance of Jerusalem to err, and to do worse than the heathen, whom the LORD had destroyed before the children of Israel. And the LORD spake to Manasseh, and to his people: but* *they would not hearken. Wherefore the LORD brought upon them the captains of the host of the king of Assyria, which took Manasseh among the thorns, and bound him with fetters, and carried him to Babylon."*

As you can see, God wanted to bless His people and did bless them, but just like Adam and Eve, when they rejected the way of the LORD, He took their good life away and sent them into Hell on earth, Babylon, a type of Gehenna. But the good news is, the story does not end there. The next few verses tells us that God is a God of mercy.

Vs 12-20 *"And when he was in affliction, he besought the LORD his God, and humbled himself greatly before the God of his fathers, And prayed unto him: and he was entreated of him, and heard his supplication, and brought him again to Jerusalem into his kingdom. Then Manasseh knew that the LORD he was God. Now after this he built a wall without the city of David, on the west side of Gihon, in the valley, even to the entering in at the fish gate, and compassed about Ophel, and raised it up a very great height, and put captains of war in all the fenced cities of Judah. And he took away the strange gods, and the idol out of the house of the LORD, and all the altars that he had built in the mount of the house of the LORD, and in Jerusalem, and cast them out of the city. And he repaired the altar of the LORD, and sacrificed thereon peace offerings and thank offerings, and commanded Judah to serve the LORD God of Israel. Nevertheless the people did sacrifice still in the high places, yet unto the LORD their God only. Now the rest of the acts of Manasseh, and his prayer unto his God, and the words of the seers that spake to him in the name of the LORD God of Israel, behold, they are written in the book of the kings of Israel. His prayer also, and how God was intreated of him, and all his sin, and his trespass, and the places wherein he built high places, and set up groves and graven images, before he was humbled: behold, they are written among the sayings of the seers. So*

Manasseh slept with his fathers, and they buried him in his own house..."

I could go on and on, but I will not. Over and over again, page after page, we are treated with the stories of all those who had opportunity to benefit from God's blessed calling and commands, but time after time Gehenna became the story instead of Eden. However, when we read the story of Manasseh, we find God's willingness to forgive and grant mercy. Yet in these last verses of this life story, we see that, even though he repented and turned his life around, the ones he left behind had tendencies to stay in the life of rebellion.

When we read the story of Manasseh, we can see that if we turn we can find grace in the arms of God. One might ask, why are you telling us about these ancient kings, and how they are miserable examples of how ***not*** to live? Because they threw all their opportunities away and rejected the God that gave them so much; and He allowed them to live in a Hell on earth (a place that Jesus came along and put a name to – Gehenna)!

New Testament examples:

Judas Iscariot is one that stands out. Even though he walked with Jesus himself for over three years, he turned his direction towards Gehenna. He didn't like it there, and then tried to take himself out of it by getting out of this world. Who knows where he came to on the other side of Gehenna. Hades?

The Pharisees and scribes looked right into the face of the Messiah but gave their lives to Gehenna. Jesus introduced this word Himself as He preached, as you know. The sad story here is that they thought that they were living the greatest of lives, but Jesus exposed their misery and hypocrisy.

Jesus gave us the best story to illustrate this issue as He told the story of the Prodigal Son. Luke 15:11-24 *"And he said, A certain man had two sons: And the younger of them said to his father, Father, give me the portion of goods that falleth to me. And he divided unto them his living. And not many days after the younger son gathered all together, and took his journey into a far country, and there wasted his substance with riotous living. And when he had spent all, there arose a mighty famine in that land; and he began to be in want. And he went and joined himself to a citizen of that country; and he sent him into his fields to feed swine. And he would fain have filled his belly with the husks that the swine did eat: and no man gave unto him. And when he came to himself, he said, How many hired servants of my father's have bread enough and to spare, and I perish with hunger! I will arise and go to my father, and will say unto him, Father, I have sinned against heaven, and before thee, And am no more worthy to be called thy son: make me as one of thy hired servants. And he arose, and came to his father. But when he was yet a great way off, his father saw him, and had compassion, and ran, and fell on his neck, and kissed him. And the son said unto him, Father, I have sinned against heaven, and in thy sight, and am no more worthy to be called thy son. But the father said to his servants, Bring forth the best robe, and put it on him; and put a ring on his hand, and shoes on his feet: And bring hither the fatted calf, and kill it; and let us eat, and be merry: For this my son was dead, and is alive again; he was lost, and is found. And they began to be merry."*

As you can tell by the ins and outs of this story, our Father does not want us to live apart from Him, because living apart from Him is a second-rate life in any situation.

But there is more to this story. Jesus continued. Vs 25 *"Now his elder son was in the field: and as he came and drew nigh to the house, he heard music and dancing. And he called one of the servants and asked what these things meant. And he said unto him, Thy brother is come; and thy father hath killed the fatted calf, because he hath received him safe and sound. And he was angry, and would not go in: therefore came his father out, and entreated him. And he answering said to his father, Lo these many years do I serve thee, neither transgressed I at any time thy commandment: and yet thou never gavest me a kid, that I might make merry with my friends: But as soon as this thy son was come, which hath devoured thy living with harlots, thou hast killed for him the fatted calf. And he said unto him, Son, thou art ever with me and all that I have is thine. It was meet that we should make merry, and be glad: for this thy brother was dead, and is alive again; and was lost, and is found."*

It is clear here we have one story but two lessons. Both of the boys who belonged to this father were in a world of Gehenna! The youngest son went away to Gehenna, but the oldest boy stayed home and dwelled in Gehenna. Gehenna is not a location; Gehenna is a mindset. Gehenna is any where you are that is not in true harmony with the Father. Gehenna comes in various shapes and sizes but Gehenna is not a good place to live. Both of these boys were out of step with their father, and as much in danger of the fires of Gehenna as the one Jesus told of who called his brother a fool. This is just one story from the lips of Jesus declaring this lesson.

We must understand a very important principle in God's Word. God knows that humans have two areas that must be corrected: being out of harmony with God and being out of harmony with man. When you read the law, the Ten Commandments, they address issues with God first and man second.

Let me refresh your memory!

Exodus 20:1-20 *"And God spake all these words, saying, I am the LORD thy God, which have brought thee out of the land of Egypt, out of the house of bondage.*

1. *Thou shalt have no other gods before me.*
2. *Thou shalt not make unto thee any graven image, or any likeness of any thing that is in heaven above, or that is in the earth beneath, or that is in the water under the earth: ...*
3. *Thou shalt not take the name of the LORD thy God in vain...*
4. *Remember the sabbath day, to keep it holy...*
5. *Honour thy father and thy mother...*
6. *Thou shalt not kill.*
7. *Thou shalt not commit adultery.*
8. *Thou shalt not steal.*
9. *Thou shalt not bear false witness against thy neighbor.*
10. *Thou shalt not covet...anything that is thy neighbour's."*

Notice, the first four commandments are focused on being right with God and the last six are about treating our fellow humans right.

Remember when Jesus was asked what the greatest commandment is, He said to love the Lord thy God with all your heart, and with all your soul and with all your mind. *"This is the first and great commandment. And the second is like unto it, Thou shalt love thy neighbour as thyself. On these two commandments hang all the law and the prophets."* Matthew 22:36-40

When Jesus told the story of the Prodigal, there were two that were living in Gehenna. Then we come to one of the other stories that everyone seems to know.

The Rich Young Ruler---Luke 18:18-24 *"And a certain ruler asked him, saying, Good Master, what shall I do to inherit eternal life? And Jesus* *said unto him, Why callest thou me good? none is good, save one, that is, God. Thou knowest the commandments, Do not commit adultery, Do not kill, Do not steal, Do not bear false witness, Honour thy father and they mother. And he said, All these have I kept from my youth up. Now when Jesus heard these things, he said unto him, Yet lackest thou one thing: sell all that thou hast, and distribute unto the poor, and thou shalt have treasure in heaven: and come, follow me. And when he heard this he was very sorrowful: for he was very rich. And when Jesus saw that he was very sorrowful, he said, How hardly shall they that have riches enter into the kingdom of God!"*

The rich young ruler is also declaring that money has nothing to do with whether or not we live in Gehenna. This man was rich but he was separated from God and even though he lived in riches, in his heart he was bankrupt; therefore, he came to Jesus. Jesus said, but one thing you lack to attain the kingdom of God. When we are not living in the neighborhood of God, we are in Gehenna.

There are many, many more in the New Testament life of Jesus that we could point out; but the Pharisees, the betrayer, the rich young ruler, and the two prodigals declare the many different ways to live in Gehenna and think that you have chosen well. But choosing well and walking in God's will may be very different.

6. The other side of Gehenna -- the obedient ones

Seth was the third son of Adam and Eve. Seth replaced his brother, Abel, as the one who tried to follow God's directions as much as possible in his day. The Bible simply says about Seth, Gen. 5:3-8 *"And Adam lived an hundred and thirty years, and begat a son in his own likeness, after his image; and called his name Seth: And the days of Adam after he had begotten Seth were eight hundred years: and he* *begat sons and daughters: And all the days that Adam lived were nine hundred and thirty years: and he died. And Seth lived an hundred and five years, and begat Enos: And Seth lived after he begat Enos eight hundred and seven years, and begat sons and daughters: And all the days of Seth were nine hundred and twelve years: and he died."*

Seth's Heritage was Noah and his sons; but Seth's brother Cain, not only lived in Gehenna, but he died there, as did all his descendants.

Enoch was one of Seth's great grandsons and was a wonderful example in the beginning of the scriptures that God can get close to a human. God was so close to Enoch that he stood out among the men of his day as being close to God. God has given us a picture of a man who pleased his Creator in such a way that the God of the Heavens simply took him up to heaven. Genesis 5:21 *And Enoch lived sixty and five years, and beget Methuselah. And Enoch walked with God after he begat Methuselah three hundred years, and begat sons and daughters: And all the days of Enoch were three hundred sixty and five years: And Enoch walked with God: and he was not; for God took him."*

IT seems God and Enoch had such a relationship that this world was not good enough for Enoch, so God took him to another land.

Notice what God did when He wanted to reward someone who loved Him. He took him to His house. We have no specific word for it here, but it is the opposite of Gehenna.

Noah was a man that the Bible says found grace in the eyes of the Lord. The word here for grace is declaring favor. Noah found favor in the eyes of the LORD. In turn God warned Noah about His plan to destroy all living and begin again. He then gave him a challenge that would take him over a hundred years to complete. Yes, Noah saved his family and the rest of God's creation from destruction, and he did it by being obedient to the voice of God. I don't need to say more, but if you want to read more about this story, start reading in Genesis 6 and read through chapter 10. When you do, you will find that God made a covenant with Noah and his family. God and man have great things to say about the man who believed God, and acted on his belief to the saving of the creation.

However, we can even see that a mistake on Noah's part produced Gehenna in the life of his son, Ham.

Abraham was the one who started it all for the Israelites. God looked down and saw the whole of the human race after Noah's children had been dispersed from the tower of Babel, and chose Abraham. He chose Abraham to create a people in the world that He could bless and use as examples of blessings and cursings. From Genesis 12-50 the story of God's chosen people begins. The whole Bible declares their adventure and their eventual unity before God.

Joseph- Before I leave this section of heroes and obedient victors, I must mention one of my personal favorites, Joseph. Joseph had every right to be bitter and every right to be vengeful toward his brothers, but he chose to listen to God and realize that, what the devil meant for bad, God used for good. Joseph is one of the greatest examples of a man living as far away from Gehenna as one could get in this world. It did not start out that way, but it ended up that way, because Joseph chose to obey God. Joseph's story declared in Genesis 37-50 a long story, but worth the read.

It is no mistake that God spent so much time on Joseph. This man was sent to Egypt (Gehenna) because of the rebellion of his brothers, but he turned Gehenna into paradise by staying faithful to God.

But in the midst of the great challenges facing her she still was raised to double honor.

Joseph, Mary's betrothed, cannot be ignored. Joseph probably does not get the credit he deserves for being the man that he became. It is clear that Joseph was like all other men when he heard of Mary's pregnancy, but the dream he had brought him the truth about the pregnancy, and he surrendered to the words of the angel in the dream and the words of Mary. I am sure that Joseph had many of his friends, family and even strangers give him a hard time, as he accepted Mary and her story, but Joseph walked a walk of faith. On the night when Jesus was born, Joseph saw his first signs that he was right, as the shepherds showed up at the manger and the angels were singing (and even later as the strangers from the east sought him out and gave him the gifts that they brought). The second dream of direction to take the baby and go to Egypt because of the coming assassins was further reassurance, and as he was in Egypt I am sure he heard of the death of the many children in Bethlehem after he left. Joseph had to walk a walk of faith in order to see all of this. As we use the words, "Walk the walk of faith," we are saying that we obeyed the word of God and in turned lived a life outside of Gehenna.

Zacharias and Elizabeth were the friends and kin of Mary, and God gave them the wonderful blessing of being part of the greatest story on earth ever told. They were not able to have a child, and there were many who could have been part of the Christmas story, but God saw the obedience of this priest and chose to allow him to raise the forrunner of Jesus the Christ. God sent the message to Zacharias and Elizabeth and because of Zacharias' unbelief, God gave him a little taste of Gehenna by taking one of the blessings of life, his speech. Zacharias lost his ability to speak for 9 months, and when the baby came, the first words that Zacharias spoke were after he wrote words of obedience. God told them to name the child John and God loosened his tongue after he set the record straight. The friends of Zacharias and Elizabeth were questioning her desire to name the child John. Zacharias wrote on a tablet, "His name is John," and then God ended his small visit to Gehenna and his speech returned.

Many other New Testament believers came to be a part of God's blessing, and as Jesus walked among the people of His day, He found and highlighted many that walked in the blessing of God, even though they were oppressed in their own land.

Mary Magdalene was in Gehenna in a life of prostitution. We don't know how she got there, but she was there. Jesus reached into her world and delivered her from her Hell on earth, and gave her a life in obedience to God through Jesus Christ.

The Gadarene Demonic is mentioned in Mark chapter 5. Jesus made it a point to cross the Sea of Galilee to rescue this man from Gehenna on earth. His Gehenna was extreme, but Gehenna no doubt. He was Satan-controlled and trying to destroy himself, and Jesus came to rescue him and change his life. When the town came out to see what had happened, they saw a man sitting clothed before Jesus (in control) and desiring to go with Jesus where ever he went. This deliverance brought a reaction of obedience and rejecting the Hell on earth that Gehenna brought to him.

Samaritan woman at the well - John records in Chapter 4 of the gospel of John that Jesus made it a point to travel through Samaria and to be at Jacob's well at noon that day. He knew that this woman living a life in Gehenna would be set free if she would believe in who He is and surrender to His will. She could get beyond all that she knew about religion and enter a valid relationship with Him that would change the course of her life. She stepped out of Gehenna that day and surrendered to the will of God for her life. What was her life?

She was continually trying to find a man to meet her needs and in turned lived a life full of disappointment, but Jesus came and delivered her from Hell on earth (Gehenna).

I could go on; I could talk about the Pharisees Jesus addressed and tried to help realize that they were living in Hell on earth. We have already mentioned Matthew 23:15 *"Woe unto you, scribes and Pharisees, hypocrites! for ye compass sea and land to make one proselyte, and when he is made, ye make him twofold more the child of hell (Gehenna) than yourselves."*

Nicodemus and Joseph of Arimathea were two who showed signs of coming away from the blindness of the Pharisees and beginning to live in obedience to God through first believing in Jesus, the Christ. This is the beginning, but only the beginning. Then we must begin to yield our lives unto the obedience of God's word. The sad thing was that these two men thought that they had yielded themselves to the word of God, but sadly not so much. The Pharisees in the day of Jesus were living in a world of rules apart from relationship.

The Apostle Paul found out the same thing, as Jesus rescued him from these rules without relationship. You see, we can obey the rules of the Bible and still not know the God of the Bible; and this is what we learn as we watch Jesus confront the Pharisees of His day.

The wonderful thing that we have to help us is that we are able to learn from their mistakes. It is wonderful to walk through the Word and be able to see the troubles that always come to those who miss out on the will of God in the Word of God. There have been many who have taken the words of the Bible and twisted them to place people in bondage rather than set them free. Paul discovered this and wrote to the church at Corinth in 2 Cor. 3:17, saying, *"...where the Spirit of the Lord is, there is liberty."* Freedom is the wonder of the walk of faith, not bondage. To be in bondage by God's Word is a form of Gehenna, and Satan really does a good job of taking the wonderful things that God gives us to set us free and twisting it to place us in Gehenna prison. The Pharisees were the greatest of all pictures of this. Jesus had more trouble with this group on earth than any other people, including the Romans.

It is also important to know that the taking into heaven by what Paul refers to as the taking away event (rapture) is the reversal of the putting away. When we read of Enoch on the first pages of the Bible, God gave us an example of what He desires to do. The Bible says that Enoch had such a relationship with God that God just took him home with Him; Enoch did not even die. This is an example of what will happen to the Church that is called out and are not put through the pains of death. Only Enoch and Elijah had this experience in the Old Testament, but we are told that this will happen in an instant to the ones that are a part of God through Jesus Christ. What a thing to long for!

1 Thessalonians 4:13-5:11 *"But I would not have you to be ignorant, brethren, concerning them which are asleep, that ye sorrow not, even as others which have no hope. For if we believe that Jesus died and rose again, even so them also which sleep in Jesus will God bring with him. For this we say unto you by the word of the Lord, that we which are alive and remain unto the coming of the Lord shall not prevent them which are asleep. For the Lord himself shall descend from heaven with a shout, with the voice of the archangel, and with the trump of God: and the dead in Christ shall rise first: Then we which are alive and remain shall be caught up together with them in the clouds, to meet the Lord in the air: and so shall we ever be with the Lord. Wherefore comfort one another with these words. But of the times and the seasons, brethren, ye have no need that I write unto you. For yourselves know perfectly that the day of the Lord so cometh as a thief in the night. For when they shall say, Peace and safety; then*

sudden destruction cometh upon them, as travail upon a woman with child, and they shall not escape. But ye, brethren, are not in darkness, that that day should overtake you as a thief. Ye are all the children of light, and the children of the day: we are not of the night, nor of darkness. Therefore let us not sleep, as do others; but let us watch and be sober. For they that sleep sleep in the night; and they that be drunken are drunken in the night. But let us, who are of the day, be sober, putting on the breastplate of faith and love; and for an helmet, the hope of salvation. For God hath not appointed us to wrath, but to obtain salvation by our Lord Jesus Christ, Who died for us, that, whether we wake or sleep, we should live together with him. Wherefore comfort yourselves together, and edify one another, even as also ye do."

1 Corinthians 15:51-54 "Behold I shew you a mystery; We shall not all sleep, but we shall all be changed, In a moment, in the twinkling of an eye, at the last trump: for the trumpet shall sound, and the dead shall be raised incorruptible, and we shall be changed. For this corruptible must put on incorruption, and this mortal must put on immortality. So when this corruptible shall have put on incorruption, and this mortal shall have put on immortality, then shall be brought to pass the saying that is written, Death is swallowed up in victory."

These verses are well known by those who are seasoned Christians, but for those who might not know about them, I have placed them in the manuscript. This is God's reversal of putting away and God's way of removing us from the briars and problems of this world, but this is only for those who are in Christ. This is a good time to encourage all readers to make sure that they have trusted in the death, burial and resurrection of Jesus Christ. It is important that we all put our trust in the finished work of the Lamb of God, Jesus the Christ. Those will be the ones taken from this briar patch, however thorny it is, to the portals of God's Personal presence.

Enoch was taken up Genesis 5:21-24 *"And Enoch lived sixty and five years, and begat Methuselah: And Enoch walked with God after he begat Methuselah three hundred years, and begat sons and daughters: And all the days of Enoch were three hundred and sixty and five years; And Enoch walked with God: and he was not; for God took him."*

2 Kings 2:11-12 records that God took His prophet Elijah into the heavens with a chariot of fire. As we have noted, God has only taken two Old Testament saints up without dying. But the Bible says that for those who know Jesus, they might be able to receive this blessing was well. Why, you may ask, is this writer including this? Because as God is disappointed in those who reject Him and rebel against Him, He puts them away into briars outside Eden, into Gehenna in the trash heaps of life and into Hades and eventually into the Lake of Fire. But for those who respond in repentance and obedience, God calls us close to Him and even takes us into His house; and He makes a big deal of this in Revelation 21:1-3 *"And I saw a new heaven and a new earth: for the first heaven and the first earth were passed away; and there was no more sea. And I John saw the holy city, new Jerusalem, coming down from God out of heaven, prepared as a bride adorned for her husband. And I heard a great voice out of heaven saying, Behold, the tabernacle of God is with men, and he will dwell with them, and they shall be his people, and God himself shall be with them, and be their God."*

We must understand that the issue of God and man is all about relationships. It is not about Heaven or Hell. It is not about Eden or the briars or Gehenna or the Promised Land. It is about being with God (or at least being close to God) or being far from Him. Death and Hell are all about being sent away.

This is why the statement is made by Jesus in Matthew 7:21-23, *"Not every one that saith unto me, Lord, Lord, shall not enter into the kingdom of heaven; but he that doeth the will of my Father which is in heaven. Many will say to me in that day, Lord, Lord, have we not prophesied in thy name? and in thy name have cast out devils? and in thy name done many wonderful works? And then with I profess unto them, I never knew you: depart from me, ye that work iniquity."*

You see, it is all about relationship. Those who come into God's circle are those who have done the Father's will. What is the Father's will? Apparently is is to get to know the Son of God; then you have done the Father's will and you will be allowed into the Father's presence.

It is consistent from cover to cover. Those who know God and are known of God are invited to God; those who do not know Him and do not obey His will are put away. It is a reward to be invited into His presence. God uses the briars of life to let us know that we are not in heaven, and He uses Gehenna to declare that we are not in obedience to the Kingdom teachings.

That is what this book is all about!

7. Examples of Gehenna in modern times

Many people are raised in countries where the whole country has been taken in a direction of Gehenna. Many travel into countries and help those who are living in conditions that are simply unimaginable. One might ask, "How did this country get in this shape?" With a little research into history, it is discovered the condition of the country is created by a few decisions made by influential people; making the heritage of the country like Gehenna. When you drive through the villages and see how the people there live, it is amazing that they continue to stay there. The truth is, many of them do not know that better can be had. We are living in times where people are seeing the world through many different platforms and publications. The world that is living in Gehenna is noticing that everyone doesn't live in Gehenna, so they are trying to go where the opportunities are different. The opportunities are different because a few influential people made some God-driven decisions and placed the foundation of their country in God's hands, and a world outside Gehenna was born. One might say that this writer is talking about America, and I would say yes I am, but it is not just America that has these opportunities. When studying history, it wasn't very long ago the western world of Europe was also such a land. A few influential leaders took the countries away from God, however, and the world began to take on Gehenna traits. Even now, America has influential people that are taking America into the out-skirts of Gehenna. Many of our cities and even states are living in Gehenna; and some cities have a Gehenna section of the city. This writer is trying to help the reader understand that this is the Gehenna effect that Jesus was talking about in His Sermon on the Mount. If we live in harmony with God's personality of kindness, care, selflessness and love, Gehenna cannot be created. But if and when we depart from the culture of Jesus, Gehenna is the outcome.

When I was a young child I remember watching a movie called "Mutiny on the Bounty." This story interested me and when I was researching for this book I looked up the true story that will illustrate what I am asserting here.

THE TRUE STORY OF THE MUTINY ON THE BOUNTY

Author: Dr. Guy Jackson

November 01, 2019

> Nothing can have a greater impact on human history, on the world, and upon individuals' lives than the Word of God, as

God's Spirit uses it to witness the truth of Jesus Christ to the hearts of people one at a time. And perhaps no story illustrates this truth more than the story of the mutiny on the bounty. Have you ever heard "the rest of the story?"

The Bounty was a British ship that set sail from England in 1787, bound for the South Seas. The idea was that those on board would spend some time among the islands, transplanting fruit-bearing trees, and doing other things to make the islands more inhabitable. After ten months of voyage, the Bounty arrived safely at its destination, and for six months, the officers and the crew gave themselves to the duties placed upon them by their government.

When the special task was completed, however, and the order came to embark again, the sailors rebelled. They had formed strong attachment for the native girls, and the climate and the ease of the South Sea island life were much to their liking. The result was a mutiny on the bounty, and the sailors placed Captain Bligh and a few loyal men adrift on the open seas in a small boat. Captain Bligh, in an almost miraculous fashion, survived the ordeal, was rescued, and eventually arrived home in London to tell his story. An expedition was launched to punish the mutineers, and in due time fourteen of them were captured and paid the penalty under British law.

But nine of the mutineers had taken the Bounty and set out to find a place where they could hide. Mutiny was, after all, a capital offense. Twelve Polynesian women, six Polynesian men, and one infant joined them. After months of exploration, they found Pitcairn Island, which had no people, but an abundance of coconuts, breadfruit, and other useful crops. The group destroyed the Bounty, to avoid detection by passing ships, and settled into their paradise.

Like the first Paradise, however, this one featured hidden dangers. Unfettered sexuality provoked jealousies and rage. The root of the ti plant, one mutineer discovered, could be distilled into liquor; and they began to make their own moonshine. The underlying problem, though, was building a society with criminals, concubines, and malcontents. Within four years, all of the Polynesian men and half of the mutineers had been murdered. A few years later, only one Englishman (Alexander Smith) remained, along with some fearful women and children.

This is where the story really begins. While poking through the items saved from the ship, Smith discovered a Bible. It was new to him. He had never read a Bible. He began to read it, and the divine power of God's Word reached into the heart of the hardened murderer on a tiny volcanic speck in the vast Pacific Ocean—and changed his life forever. The peace and love that Smith found in the Bible entirely replaced the old life of quarreling, brawling, and liquor. He began to teach the women and children form the Bible until every person on the island had experienced the same amazing change that he had found.

In 1808 (20 years after the mutiny), an American ship (the USS Topas) discovered Pitcairn Island. The crew of the Topas was shocked to find a miniature Utopia---a community of 35 English-speaking Christians living in decency, prosperity, harmony, and peace. There was no crime, disease, immorality, insanity, or illiteracy. How was it accomplished? By reading , believing, and practicing the Word of God!

The Americans reported their find, and six years later, a British ship rediscovered Pitcairn. Although the crew had orders to seize and kill any mutineer they found in the South Pacific, they couldn't bring themselves to disrupt the peaceful community by punishing Smith, now known by all on the island as "father." In fact, no one came to seize him, and he died on the island in 1829.

And even to this day, the effects continue. At the time of the writing of this article, with the population of slightly less than 100, nearly every person on Pitcairn Island is a Christian. The island originally settled by criminals and fugitives from the law has a courthouse, but it has never held a trial. Pitcairn's three jail cells house only life jackets.

This is the motivation and inspiration behind WORDview Ministries. This is why our motto is, "Read the Bible, change your world."

(This story Adapted from "Mutiny and Redemption" by Elesha Coffman, Associate Editor of Christian History, and from several other sources. GJ).

This is wonderful example of how those living in Gehenna, by God's transformation power, moved the whole community out of Gehenna and into a city built by God's Word and His mercy!

As we read stories like this from history, we discover that living in Gehenna is devastating on everyone. I discovered a story that declares this truth.

Living in Gehenna is hard on a human.

I once read the story of Leonardo Da Vinci, the popular painter of the late 1400s and early 1500s, and it is said that he would search for months and even years to find the right model who would give him the proper personalities as he was going to paint each of the Lord's disciples. It is said that it took him 20 years to finish this one painting because he was so particular as he chose the right look for each personality. It is said that he looked for a few years to find Judas Iscariot. Judas Iscariot was the very last one that he put into this painting, and he had a hard time finding a model for Judas. After a deep search, he eventually went to the local prison to see if maybe a model could be found there. He did find a man and asked the man to model for him but the man would not speak to Mr. Da Vinci. He finally went to the warden of the prison to see if he would allow this man to model for him. The warden agreed, and so the prison guards would bring this man to sit and Da Vinci would paint him. When he finally finished the painting, he asked the model to come over and see what the painting looked like to see if maybe the man would say something. When the model walked over in chains and looked at the painting, he was overwhelmed with emotion and began to cry in an extreme way. Da Vinci asked, "Sir, what is wrong, what is wrong?" The model looked up at Mr. Da Vinci and said, "Sir, do you not know?" Mr. Da Vinci said, "No I do not, can you tell me?" The model looked into the eyes of the painter and said, "I am the same model that you used 20 years ago. I was your model when you painted Jesus. "

The model made some bad decisions and apparently found himself in Gehenna. This story paints a picture of its own. One or two bad decisions can change the direction of a person's life in an amazing way to the good or to the bad. The countenance of the model had changed so much that the artist did not even recognize him.

When we think of Gehenna, we might think of Hollywood and/or the music industry. We can see hundreds and even thousands of people who once were on a path to fame and fortune, but one bad decision took him or her down a road to an early grave or even suicide. I could name names of very well-known stars whose lives ended in tragic ways. Marilyn Monroe, Michael Jackson, even Elvis Presley, all beloved people that lived glamorous lives in the public, but had private lives that were far from heavenly. Each was very beloved, but their lives were tragic and ended in tragic ways. Decisions that set their lives on courses of destruction resulted in them living in misery, and this is what Jesus called Gehenna.

Some very prominent and famous men of God who were very beloved among the world of listeners, who at a glance seemed to be heaven on earth, in the end turned into what Jesus referred to as Gehenna, because of one bad decision that could not be reversed. Some ended up in prison, some in a court room and others shamed with ministries lost. I knew a young man many years ago, when I was just getting started in the ministry. I was in college, and there was a very prominent minister that I knew there that was one of the most blessed church in the town. The man went into the Valley of Gehenna when he separated from his wife and brought another woman to the church, saying that God had given her to him instead of his wife. He was trying to live in Eden, but lived in the rebellion of Gehenna. The church accepted it, but the ministry began to fail and the man got very sick and died. Two years after he moved to Gehenna, he died. I am not saying where he will spend eternity, but for a time he lived in Gehenna (hell on earth) but not for long.

We must understand this teaching of Jesus. Our enemy, the devil, has done a good job of keeping this misunderstanding before those who read the Bible. If we understand that this is the teaching of God from the beginning pages of the Bible and remains the teaching of

God throughout the New Testament, we can see clearly why we are in the place that we are in, even though we are believers. This must be taught!

It is not hard to find a picture of living outside of the Valley of Gehenna in modern times. We look at the many marriages of people who first fell in love with Jesus, and then fell in love with the right mate, and gave their heart to God and to the right person of the opposite sex. They set their heart to serve God and each other and in the midst of life made God's word their guiding light as the scripture says in Psalms 119:105 *"Thy word is a lamp unto my feet, and a light unto my path."* As we have learned, every human being has an old sinful nature, and we all fight with the flesh to stay surrendered to God's will over our own. If we successfully navigate through life and stay away from Gehenna, we make Gods' Word part of our mental, spiritual and living DNA. It can be done, but those who have tried to live the life that I just described have battled day to day to stay on the right road. Staying out of Gehenna is simple, really, walking with God as Enoch did. That is easy to say but hard to do, and it is hard to do because of one thing: self. Also, it is important to note that when I bring another person into my world in order for me to live outside of Gehenna, they too must be willing and driven not to be pulled into this valley either. Then when we have children, they too will be tempted to pull the whole family into Gehenna. Therefore, life here is a life of victory when we die to self and live unto God. It is possible, but only if we can die to self and link up with those who also die to self. Not as simple as we thought. It is life outside the Garden of Eden, but remember, even in the garden of paradise there was temptation. Eve found that the problem came when she decided to put herself over the others in her life, like Adam, God and their future together.

It is important to note that there is a decision to make, but we do have the ability to make many of these decisions. Being born outside of the garden was not our decision and being born to a certain race or a certain sex or to a certain family was not our choice. There are many choices that we do not get to make, but the choice to put self first over other is your choice and mine. This is what puts us in Gehenna or not. That is the question.

8. Can a Christian be a believer and live in Gehenna?

We have already talked about the bondage that the Pharisees found themselves in by taking the word of God and enslaving people. It is true that our enemy, the devil, is good at twisting the Word of God to cause us pain and imprisonment. Adam and Eve found out just how good Satan is at using the earth's resources to entangle us in disobedience. He can twist the words of God in a way that makes them sound true, and in turn cause the people of God to make bad decisions, either while offended at God or thinking they are serving God while doing wrong. Remember what Jesus said to His disciples about the days ahead in *John 16:2-3 "They shall put you out of the synagogues: yea, the time cometh, that whosoever killeth you will think that he doeth God service. And these things will they do unto you, because they have not known the Father, nor me."*

We must understand that Satan is very good at confusing even the followers of God. There are literally thousands of denominations (so called) that claim to be telling the truth. The leaders of these groups may be right in some areas and wrong in others, but most do not mean to lead people astray. Whether intending to do so or not, however, if we are not in harmony with God in all areas, we are leading folks down a road of Gehenna in one or another. This is why it is so important not to deviate from the Word of God. We must carefully read and understand the New Testament apostles, as God used them to set us on the paths to deliverance and freedom, and not on the road to bondage and error. This is what the rest of the New Testament is about. We have four declarations of what Jesus came to say and do, and the book of Acts that declares the creation of the New Testament Church. Then we have the rest of the New Testament. We read from Romans to Revelation, and these books are the helpers of the followers of Christ. When we see churches and preachers get into trouble, many times they have decided to disregard the teachings of these apostles. The end result is bad, Gehenna of the Church body even.

Remember chapters 2 and 3 of the book of Revelation. Here Jesus made declarations to these churches that were getting it right and getting it wrong (and when they were getting it wrong they were experiencing the Gehenna of being wrong).

Gehenna comes in various forms and levels, depending on just how far wrong we choose to allow ourselves to live. But it is clear that obedience produces blessings and disobedience puts us into Gehenna.

1 Corinthians 9:27 *"But I keep under my body, and bring it into subjection: lest that by any means, when I have preached to others, I myself should be a castaway."*

9. Can a non-Christian live a life apart from Gehenna?

Yes it can be done. Israel is the greatest example of that. They rejected the Savior, Jesus Christ, and will miss heaven if they also individually reject the call of the Holy Spirit to them to be born again. Jesus made that abundantly clear to Nicodemus in John 3. But the

Jewish people can and have been able to be scattered into many nations. Even in the middle of great oppression they have been able to prosper, but we must understand that they prosper because of the principles of the Old Covenant. The Old Covenant law that Moses gave to them gave them the principles of prosperity.

Many humans can "borrow" principles from the Bible, do the right thing and put together a pretty good life. But any life apart from total harmony with God is second rate. I know that no human besides Jesus Himself lived totally in harmony with God's will, but when we do the best we can, the blessings of God come to us in powerful ways. We must understand that God has a perfect will, and no human is going to get it right all the time. The sin nature is constantly calling us into rebellion against God's will for our lives. Even the great servant Paul tried to explain in Romans 7:14-25 that we all are having a hard time serving God totally. As he said, *"...the law [of God] is spiritual: but I am carnal..."* He made it clear that in our flesh we are week and cannot obey God totally, but we are to aim at perfection even though we will know that it is impossible for us to hit it. Jesus told us in the Sermon on the Mount recorded in Matthew 5:48, *"Be ye therefore perfect, even as your Father which is in heaven is perfect."* If we do a study of how many times in the New Testament writings we are told to aim at perfection it will amaze us, but we get great comfort in knowing that Paul said that even he struggled with doing the right thing. You might ask, if God knows that we cannot live perfectly, why then does He tell us to aim at perfection? This writer is trying to help you understand that God knows that any deviation from perfect will produce some form or level of Gehenna, and He does not want that for our lives. So He tells us to aim at the target; and even if we miss, hopefully it's only by a little.

Think of the young lady who has a baby out of wedlock. The road that she has chosen because of previous choices made by her or for her by others may not be good, but it can be worse if she continues to make decisions outside of God's will for her life. The child that comes into her life can be a wonderful blessing (and in most cases it goes that way) but it could have been so much better if she could have brought a child into the world with God's anointed will of courting, marrying and then having the child.

Even if a young man or a young woman does not have a child out of God's order and design, if they become sexually active before they give themselves to the person of their dreams, they live their life haunted by previous lovers and relationships that they can never erase. There are some things that we do that have no reverse. We can live with many things, but every deviation from the perfect will of God for your life will produce an element of Gehenna; and we never know just how large this Gehenna affect will be. I once counseled a couple, and the young lady had had 9 other lovers before this man who was about to marry her. I did not ask for this information, but it came out of the mouth of the young lady and she could not take it back (just like she could not take back even one of these sexual encounters) no matter how hard she might try. Once her husband-to-be heard this, it changed his focus. Even after they married they did not stay married. The Valley of Gehenna affect was large in that relationship and the smell of the past plagued their future.

A young man who choses to start drinking or smoking at 15 because of peer pressure has no idea that, by the time he is 55 years old, most men that smoke for 40 years have done such damage to their lungs that breathing becomes a labor. One of the most miserable bodies to live in is one that cannot get enough air. He spends days and nights trying to satisfy the need to breathe. COPD, Cancer or any other name that comes with it: the real name should be Gehenna!

This is just a simple example of the point to be made here. It is not easy to obey God in all areas of our lives, but any deviation from God's design will bring us a certain level of Gehenna. This is the goal of this material – to help you avoid that!

One of my closest friends when I grew up was living in a world of selfishness and self-destruction, but hearing a radio broadcast he pulled over on the side off the road, cried out for God's mercy and was gloriously saved. After that, he was no longer on the destructive course that he once lived. But out of all the things he changed, he still kept smoking cigarettes. Yes, his life changed and his family changed and the life God gave him in Christ was wonderful, but still he did not stop smoking. When he got lung cancer and died, he still lost years of blessings that he would have had if he just had changed that area of his life when he came to Christ. You see, we can live our lives in God's Kingdom on earth, but any area in which we cling to the world will bring a certain amount of Gehenna to us, wherever we are.

These are just a few of the pictures of people's lives that I hope will encourage us to find our way out of any area around Gehenna.

10. What are the keys to staying out of Gehenna?

God instructed Adam and Eve in the Garden to be obedient and not to eat what He had declared off limits. God instructed that if they did what He said not to do, death would follow. They did not know what death would be or how it would, be but God said it would come. Death to God was more than one's spirit leaving the body. Death, to God, was the separation of man from the Garden of Eden; but even bigger than that, it was their separation from the ability to be in God's presence. God had to put them out of the Garden, and God could not walk in the cool of the day with them any more. That is why it was such a big deal when Jesus said that, when we believe and obey, the Comforter would come to us and be with us. John 14:15-16 *"If ye love me, keep my commandments. And I will pray the Father and he shall give you another Comforter that he may abide with you forever."* The issue was bigger than being put into the briars of life outside the Garden of Eden, they would be separated from the ability to be in God's presence. That is the real death! Even in Revelation 21 He tells us of the second death which is the last separation, when the rebels are put into the lake of fire forever. The reason it is the second death is because the first death was separation from God. When a person dies the first time the death is that they are sent into the abode of the dead (Hades), and in turn separated from God. In the second death, the issue is not so much the fire (even though that is an issue); the real second death is the separation. This time it is a forever separation.

God told Joshua in Joshua 1:6-8 that obedience is the key to being in the blessing of God, even though we live in this world of briars. *"Be strong and of good courage: for unto this people shalt thou divide for an inheritance the land, which I sware unto their fathers to give them. Only be thou strong and very courageous, that thou mayest observe to do according to all the law, which Moses my servant commanded thee: turn not from it to the right hand or to the left, that thou mayest prosper whithersoever thou goest. This book of the law shall not depart out of thy mouth; but thou shalt meditate therein day and night, that thou mayest observe to do according to all that is written therein: for then thou shalt make thy way prosperous, and then thou shalt have good success."*

The key to staying out of Gehenna is repentance. Repentance is also the key to staying out of Hades. The way to come back to God is to return to submission and come away from rebellion! Repentance is a word that declares sorrow and rejection of past decisions, and declares a desire to go with God instead of against Him. When we become believers it is important that we do repent. It is no accident that John the Baptist and Jesus' first sermons were on repentance. Matthew 3:1-2 *"In those days came John the Baptist, preaching in the wilderness of Judaea, And saying Repent ye: for the kingdom of heaven is at hand."*

When giving help to those discovering that they are in the valley of Gehenna in life, we must start with repentance, because the direction and life choices up to that point have brought them into the trash heap of life. The only way to get out of the Gehenna affect is to repent and go in another direction. Repent of bad decisions, bad attitudes and many other things that cause rebellion and walking in a direction away from God's way. It is vital that we start here!

Luke 13:1- 3 *There were present at that season some that told him of the Galilaeans, whose blood Pilate had mingled with their sacrifices. And Jesus answering said unto them, Suppose ye that these Galilaeans were sinners above all the Galilaeans, because they suffered such things? I tell you, Nay: but, except ye repent, ye shall all likewise perish."*

In Luke 15:7, Jesus told His disciples that heaven celebrated when one person repents. Many of us talk about the celebration that takes place when one person comes to God in salvation, but Jesus was making a bigger point here. He was talking not only about coming to God in salvation, but in repentance. This is the story of the shepherd that leaves the 99 sheep and goes to find the 1 sheep that has gone astray. When we realize the price of going astray, we realize why this was such a big deal. The future of that straying sheep was very bad as long as it was on its own path, not in the fold and on the shepherd's path. We must understand why that one sheep was gone. It was gone because it decided to drift away from the fold and from the shepherd. Therefore, even heaven rejoices when repentance takes place because all in heaven know the price of rebellion against God, our chief Shepherd.

In Matthew 3:8, John the Baptist even said that they needed to show that they were repenting before he would baptize them. *"Bring forth therefore fruits meet for repentance."* John knew that repentance (turning from and turning to) was the key to becoming part of this Kingdom that Jesus had come to bring to us.

Repentance is one of the key words of those who are running from Gehenna!

Submission - At the center of sin is one letter "i." When one commits rebellion against God, he or she will first put themselves before God and others. When Eve was about to choose the way of the serpent, she had to come to a place where she put herself over everyone and everything. Even Adam was put second to her desires as she took the fruit. Therefore, we must submit to God's will over our own. Submission may seem like a small thing, but if we are to have a happy home (as Paul said in Ephesians 5), we must submit ourselves one to another in the fear of God. This means we are to submit to one another as we submit to God. Submission of will is vital if we are going to be successful in our quest to repent.

Selflessness - Jesus said in Matthew 6:24-34 *"No man can serve two masters: for either he will hate the one, and love the other; or else he will hold to the one, and despise the other. Ye cannot serve God and mammon. Therefore I say unto you, Take no thought for your life, what ye shall eat, or what ye shall drink; nor yet for your body, what ye shall put on. Is not the life more than meat, and the body than raiment? Behold, the fowls of the air: for thy sow not, neither do they reap, nor gather into barns; yet your heavenly Father feedeth them. Are ye not much better than they? Which of you by taking thought can add one cubit unto his stature? And why take ye thought for* *raiment? Consider the lilies of the field, how they grow; they toil not, neither do they spin: And yet I say unto you, That even Solomon in all his glory was not arrayed like one of these. Wherefore, if God so clothe the grass of the field, which to day is, and to morrow is cast into the oven, shall he not much more clothe you, O ye of little faith? Therefore take no thought saying what shall we eat? Or what shall we drink? Or, Wherewithal shall we be clothed? (For after all these things do the Gentiles seek:) for your heavenly Father knoweth that ye have need of all these things. But seek ye first the kingdom of God, and his righteousness; and all these things shall be added unto you. Take therefore no thought for the morrow: for the morrow shall take thought for the things of itself. Sufficient unto the day is the evil thereof."*

Jesus made it clear that, if we are going to be selfless, we must be full of faith and dependency on God; and there is also a word here that needs to be mentioned: contentment. We must be content with God's provision, and not be trying to go outside of God's will to get what He does not want us to have (because it is not good for us, or we are not ready for it yet). Many of us want what will destroy us if we get it. Think on this statement, "The greatest temptation comes with prosperity!" When Adam and Eve were blessed, they fell to temptation. When Israel was about to get the land flowing with milk and honey, God warned them of this prosperity, because the greatest temptation is prosperity.

In order to be selfless, we must also be able to be content!

In these ten verses, Jesus says how to be selfless and also content. Jesus told those who would become part of His kingdom that they were to be the salt of the earth. They were to be the light of the world; but if they were sidetracked with self-will these two things would not come to be.

Staying out of the trap of offense is a big one - the word offense sounds like it has the word "fence" in it for a reason. When we get offended at the people God has sent into our world to help us, be instructors, and speak into our lives, we build a fence and we lose that influence. In turn, we walk down roads where we would not go if we had their influence. Remember that, as the serpent talked to Eve in the Garden of Eden, he began by telling her that God could not be trusted. He said that God was keeping her from eating from every tree in the garden. When she corrected him, he said that God did not want her to eat of this certain tree because He knew if she did, she would become as He is, a god. In short, the serpent wanted Eve to think that God did not love her as she thought. She built a fence in her mind between her and God and she ate the forbidden fruit. Eve needed to be offended in order to sin. It is amazing that sin seems to be introduced to humans after offense becomes part of the conversation. Just to name a few instances:

When the enemies in the midst of the Israelites (after leaving Egypt) were trying to get the people to turn back to Egypt, they would try to get the people to be offended at Moses and Aaron. In turn, God had to remove these trouble makers, who used offense as their tool. When Esau became the rebel that he was, he was offended at his brother and his father, so he went and married a Gentile and became what God calls a profane person. Even John the Baptist is warned not to be offended when he was in prison about to die. In Matthew 11 John was imprisoned by Herod. In the prison, he ask one of his friends to go and ask Jesus if He was the Christ, or should he look for another. Jesus responded to the question and told John that he had seen the blind receive their sight, cripples walk and lepers cleansed, the deaf hear, the dead raised up and the poor have the gospel preached to them. This alone would let John know that He was truly the Messiah, the Christ; but Jesus made one more statement. In

Matthew 11:6 Jesus said, *"And blessed is he, whosoever shall not be offended in me."* Why would Jesus say such a thing? Jesus was warning John not to be offended when He did not rescue him. John was going to die, and Jesus was not going to stop it, and Jesus did not want John to die offended at Jesus. Remember, John was the forerunner of the Messiah and his purpose had been served. We can look back and see this, but it was hard for John to see that in the moment. Yes, offense is a monster, and even John the Baptist (with who he was and all he knew) was tempted to get caught up in the world of offense.

Offense, this writer believes, is the monster that causes more destruction to relationships, families and especially the church family than any other singular issue. There are so many people that get offended at something the church leader, or members either did or did not do, said or did not say, then run away and blame the church for their not serving God. There are so, so many stories that this writer could tell you of people that get mad at the world of denomination, Church, preachers, and even just people that are affiliated with a church and in turn will not do anything with the evangelism arm of God or the church. In turn, many will not be reached and many will not serve because of offense. This writer believes that offense is the greatest monster in the church age. This thing called offense steals so much from God's productivity. If we could remove offense for our Christian world, we would see so much done that is not being done now. There would be so many sins that would be eliminated from the world simply because as you and I observe life, so many sin acts are preceded by offense. Young people demonize their parents before they become rebels. Husbands and wives both demonize their spouse before they are unfaithful to them. There are many aspects of sin, but offense seems to be present when sin shows up. Whatever the sin, offense seems to precede it, and when sin is committed, some even go so far as to blame the one that they were offended at for their sin.

We could say more, but it is a simple truth: if we are going to stay away from Gehenna, we must watch out for the trap of offense.

Humility - The words of Solomon as he received the throne of Israel will give us much to think about. We have already highlighted them, but I encourage you to read them again. When Solomon became the King of Israel, God asked him what he wanted on that day. Instead of asking for wealth, fame, health and long life, Solomon asked for the wisdom that he would need to do what God had called him to do; and in this request God was blessed. God responded that, because Solomon did not ask for selfish things, he would get the wisdom that he needed, and the fame, wealth and health that he did not ask for. Solomon would have done well to have stayed in that mindset, because when he left humility, he ended up in arrogance and spent the rest of his life in a world that Jesus would have called Gehenna.

When Jesus started His work on the earth, He started with a few choice words. These were and are words that introduce those who are going to be part of His kingdom on earth and later in heaven. We can mention words and attitudes that will help us stay out of Gehenna, but Jesus laid out the qualities that it would take to stay out of Gehenna and participate in His invasion on the earth. Yes, Jesus came and invaded the earth with His teachings and He was recruiting soldiers to carry out His kingdom invasion. When you read these words I believe that you can see that Jesus used them to introduce to us what I am calling, "the Gehenna Code." Jesus introduced this word right after He introduced His Kingdom and His Kingdom principles. Let's take a look!

Matthew 5:3-20 ""Blessed are the poor in spirit: for theirs is the kingdom of heaven. Blessed are they that mourn: for they shall be comforted. Blessed are the meek: for they shall inherit the earth. Blessed are they which do hunger and thirst after righteousness: for they shall be filled. Blessed are the merciful: for they shall obtain mercy. Blessed are the pure in heart: for they shall see God. Blessed are the peacemakers: for they shall be called the children of God. Blessed are they which are persecuted for righteousness sake: for theirs is the kingdom of heaven. Blessed are ye, when men shall revile you, and persecute you, and shall say all manner of evil against you falsely, for my sake. Rejoice and be exceedingly glad: for great is your reward in heaven: for so persecuted they the prophets which were before you. Ye are the salt of the earth: but if the salt have lost his savour, wherewith shall it be salted? It is thenceforth good for nothing, but to be cast out, and to be trodden under foot of men. Ye are the light of the world. A city that is set on a hill cannot be hid. Neither do men light a candle, and put it under a bushel, but on a candlestick; and it giveth light unto all that are in the house. Let your light so shine before men, that they may see your good works, and glorify your Father, which is in heaven. Think not that I am come to destroy the law, or the prophets: I am not come to destroy, but to fulfill. For verily I say unto you, Till heaven and earth pass, one jot or one tittle shall on no wise pass from the law, till all be fulfilled. Whosoever therefore shall break one of these least commandments, and shall teach men so, he shall be called the least in the kingdom of heaven: but whosoever shall do and teach them, the same shall be called great in the kingdom of heaven. For I say unto you, That except your righteousness exceed the righteousness of the scribes and Pharisees, ye shall in no case enter into the kingdom of heaven."

Then Jesus introduced the word Gehenna in the next segments of teaching. It seems as though He was saying that, if we are to be a part of His earthly invasion, we would need to know a few things:

1. how the ones who will be a part of His invasion will conduct themselves
2. how those who will be a part of His invasion will think
3. how those who reject His invasion will find themselves in the world of Gehenna

From verse 3 to verse 20 He set the expectations, and from verse 21 to verse 30 He explained the alternative.

Vs 21 -30 "Ye have heard that it was said by them of old time, Thou shalt not kill; and whosoever shall kill shall be in danger of the judgment: But I say unto you, That whosoever is angry with his brother without a cause shall be in danger of the judgment: and whosoever shall say to his brother, Raca, shall be in danger of the council: but whosoever shall say, Thou fool, shall be in danger of hell [Gehenna] fire. Therefore if thou bring thy gift to the altar, and there rememeberest that thy bother hath ought against thee; Leave there thy gift before the altar, and go thy way; first be reconciled to thy brother, and then come and offer thy gift. Agree with thine adversary quickly, whiles thou art in the way with him; lest at any time the adversary deliver thee to the judge, and the judge deliver thee to the officer, and thou be cast into prison. Verily say unto thee, Thou shalt by no means come out thence, till thou hast paid the uttermost farthing. Ye have heard that it was said by them of old time, Thou shalt not commit adultery: But I say unto you, That whosoever looketh on a woman to lust after her hath committed adultery with her already in his heart. And if thy right eye offend thee, pluck it out, and cast it from thee: for it is profitable for thee that one of thy members should perish, and not that thy whole body should be cast into Hell [Gehenna]. And if thy right hand offend thee, cut it off, and cast it from thee: for it is profitable for thee that one of they members should perish, and not that thy whole body should be cast into hell [Gehenna].

I have put these verses here to showcase my point. Jesus was beginning His teaching of Kingdom living, earthly and heavenly. It is important to understand that this is the context of the introduction of the word Gehenna. It is also important to study these verses carefully to understand that Jesus wanted those of us who take His Kingdom seriously to understand something: we will either become salt and light that make a difference, or we become castaways like salt or wasted light from a hidden candle. When we choose Gehenna we cannot be salt and light. It is a waste, and we fail in our purpose of becoming part of His kingdom invasion. Instead of becoming a soldier in the Kingdom invasion, we settle for a house in Gehenna.

11. How do we move out of the Valley of Gehenna once we discover that we are living there?

The previous section is one that could be put into action in order to come from Gehenna to God. Repentance is essential! We have already discussed this; but there is something that needs to take place before repentance. When one is living in Gehenna, there needs to be one thing first: confession!

Confession – One might ask, is it too late for me? I would contend that, if God in His providence brought you to this material, it is not too late for you. God is calling you to come away from the Gehenna smells and Gehenna life, but there are a few things that are necessary to walk out of Gehenna.

We have already talked about repentance. and repentance is one of the key ingredients to come away from Gehenna and back into God's favor. Let us review again a story that Jesus told us in light of this Gehenna lesson.

Luke 15:11-20 *"And he said, A certain man had two sons: And the younger of them said to his father, Father, give me the portion of goods that falleth to me. And he divided unto them his living. And not many days after the younger son gathered all together, and took his journey into a far country, and there wasted his substance with riotous living. And when he had spent all, there arose a mighty famine in that land; and he began to be in want. And he went and joined himself to a citizen of that country; and he sent him into his fields to feed swine. And he would fain have filled his belly with the husks that the swine did eat: and no man gave unto him. And when he came to himself, he said, How many hired servants of my father's have bread enough and to spare, and I perish with hunger! I will arise and go to my father, and will say unto him, Father, I have sinned against heaven, and before thee, And am no more worthy to be called thy son: make me as one of thy hired servants. And he arose, and came to his father. But when he was yet a great way off, his father saw him, and had compassion, and ran, and fell on his neck, and kissed him."*

This young man needed to come to himself before repentance could be his. He needed to confess what he had done in order to not do it again. That is why confession is such a big issue. Confession is medicine against repeating sin.

We need to begin with confession! In this story of the lost son, recorded in Luke 15, the prodigal had to come to himself before he would come to his father. This young man was in Gehenna and he was suffering what a person suffers that goes against his father and selfishly rebels. The prodigal needed to come to the end of the way of Gehenna. Once the young man walked all the way to the end of the valley of Gehenna he realized a few things as he was coming to himself. The word used in Luke 15:17 was that he came to himself, which is a word that denotes a change of direction in his life. This was the point of turning *from*, and in turn, he turned *to*.

When we turn, we must become sick of the smell of Gehenna, we must become sick of the sights of Gehenna and in turn, we will turn towards home. After he came to himself, he came to the father who was their waiting all the time. However we must note that when he returned home, though he was treated like a son, his inheritance was gone. The father told the other son that all that the father had is going to be his. Living in Gehenna is expensive! If you are reading this but still haven't had enough of the smell and misery of Gehenna, the longer you stay away, the more of life and goodness you will miss out on. Just so you know. Sin is expensive, and the longer you sit at the table of sinners, the more of your eternal wealth you are wasting. We have one opportunity to gain wealth for our King and stand at the judgment seat with rewards to offer God in Heaven when we see Him. However, if we waste our one life here on Gehenna living, we will waste the opportunities and stand before God empty handed.

Therefore, waste no more time there in Gehenna and come back to God so you will have something in your hands as you stand before God in glory.

I say this understanding that the Bible tells us that all Christians will stand before God and give an account for our lives after we are saved, whether good or bad. 2 Corinthians 5:9-10 *"Wherefore we labor, that, whether present or absent, we may be accepted of him. For we must all appear before the judgment seat of Christ; that every one may receive the things done in his body, according to that he hath done, whether it be good or bad."*

Return from the world's influence to God's

It is important to be a part of a church family for many reasons, but the best one is because we are told to be in the house of the Lord and to not stay away. It is very hard to stay out of Gehenna in any area of life, but it is even harder if we are alone, without God's family to help us. In Hebrews 10, we are told not to forsake the assembling of ourselves together. It is important to be a part of the right church family that gives us the platform to grow and exercise our faith walk being disciples.

Whether it is angels or humans, God offers Heaven on earth **and** after earth, or Hell on earth **and** after our lives on earth.

This is the story -- and what a story it is!

12. What did we learn? Conclusion!

Adam and Eve were rejected from the Garden of Eden (paradise) and sent into the world of death and danger because they did not want to be in harmony with God's word. It is amazing, but those of us who do not live in harmony with God will find ourselves in a place that is even a step down from that. Gehenna is the word for the valley of rejection. When we reject God's Word and God's way that He has given us to live, we are also sent away into the valley of Gehenna, trash.

I know that this is hard to take, but it is not hard to understand. When we reject God, He rejects us; and Hell on earth or Hell in eternity are the only options.

I think you can conclude that the Gehenna Code is throughout the Bible. God started in His first encounter with rebellion by putting Adam and Eve in a world of earthly distress. Compared to Eden, it was a world that was like a trash heap. Think about the paradise of God and the protections, pleasures and possibilities that vanished away from them after they were sent outside of the wonderful gate. This Gehenna Code is all through the Bible. Even the judgement of God in the end will be the same principle. God will be putting the rebellious away from Him in a place that is worse than here. God chose to move us away from Eden to this world. When this opportunity to re-establish our relationship is over, if we do not find God through Jesus and the gospel message, we will step even further into the separation of fire. But until then, God uses this picture of Gehenna to encourage us to be obedient and to live in harmony with God's Word. We get a sample of Hell by living in Gehenna while here on earth; but if that does not help us know that separation from God is Hell on earth then further measures are taken. We must understand that Gehenna is not judgement, but a warning to all who reject God and His will for their lives. The whole Bible, one story after another, declares this truth. We started with this as we quoted the famous words of Jeremiah in Ch. 29:11 *"For I know the thoughts that I think toward you, saith the LORD, thoughts of peace, and not of evil, to give you an expected end."* God's desire is to give us a blessed life with peace and goodness, but if we do not heed the invitation to walk with God, He will give us Hell on earth to simply let us know the future for us if we do not repent and return to the side of God. The rest of that passage in Jeremiah declares that Israel did not heed this invitation and continued in rebellion; and then we read the rest of that statement. Jeremiah 29 Verses 12-14 *"Then shall ye call upon me, and ye shall go and pray unto me, and I will hearken unto you. And ye shall seek me, and find me, when ye shall search for me with all your heart. And I will be found of you, saith the LORD: and I will turn away your captivity, and I will gather you from all the nations, and from all the places wither I have driven you, saith the LORD; and I will bring you again into the place whence I caused you to be carried away captive."* God had put Israel in the land flowing with milk and honey just as He did with Adam and Eve in the paradise of Eden, but just as Adam and Eve rejected God's direction for their lives, so did Israel. Therefore, they were sent out of the land flowing with milk and honey into the world of Gehenna. Gehenna comes in many forms but it is always a trash heap, separated from God. This is the Principle of the Gehenna Code, which is on every page of the book of God called the Holy Bible. It is all about inviting humans to live in goodness with God or live in Gehenna without Him. Notice, we said humans. This invitation is not for the angels that God had to put away. Remember the words of Jesus as He spoke to Nicodemus in John 3: man must be born again -- born of water and born of the Spirit. Why did Jesus say born of water? Two reasons: when we are born from our mother, we are born of water, as the water breaks and we are brought forth. This focuses us on the fact that we have the first birth and need a second birth to go into God's house eternally. But the second thing is that angels are not born of water; therefore, this is not an invitation to the fallen angel population. Therefore, we are invited through Jesus Christ to return to heaven with Him, but first we must be born of the Spirit and that will come when we repent of our sinful rebellion and surrender to God's will. Hence the Apostle Paul wrote to the Corinthians in *1 Corinthians 6:20 "For ye are bought with a price: therefore glorify God in your body, and in your spirit, which are God's."* And he wrote in *1 Corinthians 7:23 "Ye are bought with a price; be not ye the servants of men."*

I pray that we will understand that God does not want us living in Gehenna. God wants nothing but good for us, but we have the ability to choose where we live. We live in the promised land or outside of the promised land in Gehenna. The only question is how deep into Gehenna you or I will be building our home, depending on the amount of rebellion. Some live in the outskirts of Gehenna and some live in the depths of Gehenna, depending on our spirit of rebellion.

1 Corinthians 9:27 *"But I keep under my body, and bring it into subjection: lest that by any means, when I have preached to others, I myself should be a castaway."*

Castaway---96---Adokimos---unworthy, worthless, disapproved, one to be thrown aside...

Paul said that even he could be placed on the shelf of rebellion. This is one of the worst places to live, but we have discussed how we can return to God; by repenting. John the Baptist started the ministry of the New Covenant with these words, "Repent for the Kingdom of God is at hand." Jesus started His ministry with the same words. Therefore, we must conclude that Jesus is offering a second chance, a new birth, a new life. We can move close to God as we harmonize with His will for us, but even born again believers can live in some elements of Gehenna, depending on how big or small their repentance is.

It is a running theme all through the Bible: Eden (paradise) or briar patch -- Promised Land or Babylon -- freedom or suppression (Romans) -- Beulah Land (the marriage) or Gehenna (Trash life) -- Heaven or Hell? Any life apart from God and His will is a second rate life. It is not **whether** it is going to be dark and trashy; the only question is, **how** dark and trashy will you allow it to get?

This writer is not belittling the fires of eternal Hell (Hades), because Jesus made it clear in Luke 16 that the Rich man was in torment. Five times he said that he was tormented, making the point that he was tortured in flames. Just being separated from God for all eternity would be bad enough, but he made it clear that it was a place of eternal torment by fire. In Matthew 25:41 Jesus said that everlasting fire was prepared for the devil and his angels and really wasn't for man, but when mankind rejects God he is placed in the same category with the rebellious angels. However, humans that reject Jesus are worse than the devil and his angels. Think on this! God did not send His son to suffer at the hands of the Romans and die for the devil and his angels, but he did for His humans that were created. Therefore, if we reject the sacrifice of Jesus, we are really worse than the devil and his angels.

But Gehenna was and is a world on earth that is an alternative to God's good graces. God has made it possible for his human flesh to walk with Him and live a life in harmony with His will, blessed in life and in death. But, if we choose to reject Him by rejecting His teaching and His will for us, we reject the blessings that come with His words and His will. This is what Jesus calls Gehenna!

This writer has written this material so that all who will read and understand "the Gehenna Code" will reject a life in rebellion against God's will in every form. Life is filled with enough briars and thorns as it is, but when we reject God's word and His will we jump from the briars into the fire of Gehenna, the trash heap of life. From now on I hope you and I will identify the jail cells of rebellion, the addictions of rebellion, the divorce courts of rebellion and the conflicts of rebellion for what they are -- forms of Gehenna.

The sad thing that must be said as well is that if you and I choose to live our lives at a rebellious address of Gehenna, we take our family members and friends there to live with us. Think on this fact!

In the book of Hebrews, the writer tried to get the Jewish people to recognize their Messiah and in all of their opportunities they still, as a nation, said no. He explained to them in Chapter 12 that God had been so good to them, making them His chosen people. They had a seat to see the Messiah better than anyone else on the planet, but instead of embracing Him, they rejected Him, so he said that "they failed of the grace of God." The word grace is the word Charis, from where we get the word Charisma, "one that is favored." They were the favored ones, and they did not use their favored position to see and follow the Messiah Jesus. Therefore, they had failed the grace (favor) of God. He went on to explain that they would become bitter and not only defile themselves and others.

Hebrews 12:12-15 *"Wherefore lift up the hands which hang down, and the feeble knees; And make straight paths for your feet, lest that which is lame be turned out of the way; but let it rather be healed. Follow peace with all men, and holiness, without which no man shall see the Lord. Looking diligently lest any man fail of the grace of God; lest any root of bitterness springing up trouble you, and thereby many be defiled."*

He then used Esau as an example of Hell on earth. Esau was the first born of Isaac and in turn was to inherit the birthright and all the perks of being the grandson of Abraham and Isaac's first born. We say today that the Israelites are descendants of Abraham, Isaac and Jacob but we were supposed to say, Abraham, Isaac and Esau. One might ask, what is the big deal? But it was and is a big deal, not only for Esau's life on earth but for the life to come. Esau became very bitter, married a Gentile idol worshiper, and in turn developed a legacy that was far from God. God uses his rebellion and bitterness as an example of what not to do. God calls him a profane person and uses him as an example of one who failed the grace of God. Instead of Esau living the life of blessing that God had planned for him, he lived in Hell on earth as the writer of Hebrews said in Hebrews 12: 17. *"For ye know how that afterward, when he would have inherited the blessing, he was rejected: for he found no place of repentance, though he sought it carefully with tears".*

Esau lived and died in a place that God never intended him to be. He lived in Hell on earth, one of his own making. He lived in Gehenna on earth, the trash valley instead of the hills of Jerusalem and the Promised Land. Instead of inheriting the grace (favor) of God he endured the Hell of the Gehenna Valley. What was Esau's crime? Esau did not value God's goodness to him and gave his birthright away for a bowl of soup (savory meat). You can read this story in its fullest in Genesis 27-28. When reading Esau's story, just remember that God said Esau found no place for repentance, though he sought it with tears. This is God's way of saying that Esau had no way to turn around and go back. Esau, could not undo his rebellion and in turn lived a second rate life in a second rate place, and gave his children a second rate inheritance in this life and the life to come.

I will close out this learning adventure with the words to a song that seems to say it all. When I was a young man, I heard a country song on the radio. George Jones sang the song called "Choices" written for George by Billy Yates.

"Choices"

I've had choices, since the day that I was born
There were voices, that told me right from wrong
If I had listened, no, I wouldn't be here today
Living and dying with the choices I've made.

I was tempted, by an early age I found, I liked drinking
Oh, and I never turned it down
There were loved ones, but I turned them all away
Now I'm living and dying, with the choices I made

I've had choices, since the day that I was born
There were voices, that told me right from wrong

If I had listened, no I wouldn't be here today
Living and dying with the choices I've made

I guess I'm payin' for the things that I have done
If I could go back, oh Lord know that I would run
But I'm still losin' this game of life I play
Living and dying with the choices I made

I've had choices, since the day that I was born
There were voices, that told me right from wrong
If I had listened, no I wouldn't be here today
I'm living and dying, with the choices I made

Yes living and dying, with the choices I made!

A final word:

I want all the readers to know I understand that sometimes we find ourselves in the briar patch. I know that I have referenced the briar patch a few times in this book about Gehenna. In Genesis 3, God told Adam, Eve and the serpent that their future would be thorns and thistles.

Genesis 3:17-18 *"And unto Adam he said, Because thou hast hearkened unto the voice of thy wife, and hast eaten of the tree, of which I commanded thee, saying, Thou shalt not eat of it: cursed is the ground for thy sake; in sorrow shalt thou eat of it all the days of thy life; Thorns also and thistles shall it bring forth to thee; and thou shalt eat the herb of the field;"*

We are born in a briar patch, and there are lots of issues, troubles and situations that are in our lives simply because of the fact that we are born among thorns and thistles. Jesus knew this as well, but He also communicated that it can be a good briar patch or a bad one determined by our continual choices. Remember that a rabbit uses the briars to stay protected from the foxes. A briar patch can be a wonderful place to pick black berries, and the blooms and flowers among the thorns smell wonderful in the summer time. However, the blackberry briar patch is also a place where you will meet up with black snakes. They, too, like to be among the blackberries. This world has lots of problems, simply because it is a fallen world; but by God's grace, we have the opportunity to serve Him in these thorns and build a wonderful place of protection in these briars. But if we choose to rebel against God, the thorns turn into Gehenna. That is the rest of the story, declared by Jesus when He introduced the Gehenna concept to the world of briars.

May each reader find peace in knowledge and joy in understanding! May God work in your life in ways that will turn your briars into blackberry patches and in turn, black berry jam. May you find your way to the table that Jesus is preparing for us, as we prepare to return from the briars and step back into Eden (paradise) once again.

Gehenna Code Questions:

Chapter 1 -- Understanding Hades

1. What are the three words translated Hell in the New Testament Scriptures?

2. Why does God use three different words to describe Hell?

3. What Old Testament Hebrew word is the same as the Greek word Hades?

4. What do Sheol and Hades tell us about what happens when a non-believer dies?

5. Which passage out of the 10 passages where Hades is mentioned did this writer say tells us the most about Hades?

6. When understanding what Hades means, how does this understanding influence your thoughts when you read that Jesus said, "The gates of Hades shall not prevail against the church?"

7. When Jesus said in Revelations 1:18 that He was once dead but now alive, and holds the keys to Hades and death, discuss what this statement says, in light of what we have learned about Hades.

8. In short, Hades is the abode of the dead of the_____.

Chapter 2 -- Salvation

1. What is the Hebrew words for salvation used by Moses in Exodus 14:13, as they were about to cross the Red Sea?

2. When Adam and Eve decided to rebel against God's word, how did God respond?
3. Tell me what Adam and Eve and their rebellion have to do with the need for salvation?
4. In the story of Cain and Abel, what were the sons of Adam trying to do when Cain killed his brother?
5. In the story of Cain and Abel, why did God reject Cain's offering?
6. How did the sacrifice of Jesus on the cross fulfill Abel's salvation picture?
7. If salvation is a gift of God, what do we need to do to receive it?
8. When we understand that salvation is a gift, what could we do to have the gift taken away? Give biblical examples of anyone who has lost their eternal gift.
9. How do the statements about Hell (Gehenna) conflict with salvation being a gift?

Chapter 3 -- Understanding the Word Gehenna

1. When Jesus introduced Gehenna to the world in His sermon recorded in Matthew 5, what was Jesus trying to say?
2. When Jesus began to introduce His teaching on the mountain side, what kingdom was these principles a part of?
3. Since Gehenna is the description of the trash heap in Jerusalem, what do you think He was telling the hearers on the hillsides by using this word?
4. In Matthew 18, why is the issue of offense such a caging force for Gehenna?

5. Why did Jesus tell the scribes and Pharisees when they make a disciple, they were making a child of Gehenna just like they were and even worse?
6. When Jesus said in Mark 9:42-48 that we need to be willing to lose our eye or our hand in order to stay out of Gehenna, what does this say about Gehenna?
7. How does understanding the word Gehenna change my understanding of how to live and the price we pay, if we ignore this great teaching important for us?
8. In your own words, why is living in Gehenna such a bad thing?

Chapter 4 -- A look at the history of Gehenna

1. Where did the word Gehenna come from? Give me the word's history according to this author.
2. What did Jeremiah say about the Valley of Gehenna?
3. Why did Jeremiah call this valley the Valley of the Slaughter?
4. Why did Jeremiah call this valley the Valley of the son of Hinnom?
5. Why was this valley called the Valley of Giants?
6. What do you think His audience thought when Jesus began to use this word, seeing they had history with it?

Chapter 5 -- Examples of Gehenna in the scriptures

1. What do we believe it means when Jesus began to refer to this valley and tell people that they were in danger of this valley?
2. How did Adam and Eve live out the principles of Gehenna once they relocated outside Eden?

3. How did the life of Cain declare the principles of Gehenna?
4. What other Old Testament Characters were living their lives in Gehenna?
5. What is the one factor that causes the Old Testament saints to dwell in Gehenna?
6. Give me Two New Testament examples of those living their lives in Gehenna?
7. Why is it important to know that **both** the prodigal and his brother lived in Gehenna for a time?

Chapter 6 -- The Other side of Gehenna!

1. What makes the writer think that Seth did not live in Gehenna?
2. Why do we believe that Enoch did not live in Gehenna?
3. How did Joseph take his Gehenna life in Egypt and turn it into Eden?
4. Why does this writers believe that Daniel was able to turn Gehenna (Babylon) into Gehenna Eden?
5. Explain how Zacharias had a time in Gehenna and how he came out and back to blessings.
6. Mary Magdalene, The Gadarene Demonic, the Samaritan woman at the well: each were living in Gehenna but were set free. How did that happen?
7. How did Nicodemas and Joseph of Arimathea come out of Gehenna, and what makes us believe that they did?
8. What declaration did we discuss that will deliver all believers back to Eden (paradise) eventually?
9. Why will the non-believers be left out of that rescue?

Chapter 7 -- Examples of Gehenna in modern times!

1. How did this writer point out that many nations live in Gehenna every day?
2. Seeing we understand the principle of Gehenna, why do you believe so many are trying to come to America from many other nations?
3. How did the story of "The Mutiny on the Bounty" describe how God will use His Word to deliver a people from Gehenna if they will heed His Word?
4. In light of the principles of Gehenna, tell me why the Judas model was so upset at Leonardo Da Vinci when he did not recognize him.
5. Explain how what we have learned here compels us to make decisions in harmony with God's word.

Chapter 8 -- Can a Christian live in the Valley of Gehenna?

1. In light of what you now know, can a believing Christian be on their way to heaven and live their life on earth in Gehenna?
2. How is it possible to be saved from Hades but not be saved from Gehenna?
3. Jesus introduced Gehenna when He was teaching that His kingdom was coming down. Why is this important to know?
4. What is the key word to getting an address in the Valley of Gehenna?
5. If Gehenna comes in various forms and various levels, what determines what level we could live in?
6. Explain in your own words how a Christian can live in Gehenna but still be a Christian.

Chapter 9 -- Do all non-Christians live in Gehenna?

1. Can a non-Christian live outside of Gehenna?
2. Explain how this writer said that one who is not going to heaven could live outside Gehenna.
3. Do you believe a non-Christian can live outside of Gehenna their whole life but, end up in Hades for eternity?
4. Give me biblical examples to why you believe what you believe.
5. After reading this chapter, explain your thoughts on a non-Christian living outside of Gehenna.

Chapter 10 -- What key elements are important to keep us from living in the Valley of Gehenna?

1. What are the keys to staying out of Gehenna?
2. What does the word repentance have to do with staying out of Gehenna?
3. Why did Jesus tell His disciples that unless they and everyone else repent, all would perish?
4. Why did John the Baptist want those being baptized to show some fruit of repentance before baptism?
5. What are some of the key words this writer suggests are important for us to stay out of Gehenna?
6. Explain why this writer believes that the kingdom of God is an invasion from Heaven?
7. After reading Chapter 10, explain the invasion of the kingdom of God on to the earth.

Chapter 11 -- How do we move out of the Valley of Gehenna once we discover that we are living there?

1. What word do we start with as Jesus explained the prodigal son?
2. How is it that the prodigal son ended up in Gehenna?
3. When did the prodigal start to aim his life **out of** this Gehenna Valley?
4. Why does this writer say that **the elder son** was in Gehenna even though he stayed home and did not follow the example of his brother?
5. In this elder son's story, does this mean that Christians who serve the Father but stay angry at their brother can live in Gehenna?
6. How did the youngest son in Luke Chapter 15 get back in the father's house and out of Gehenna?
7. What could the eldest son have done to get out of or stay out of Gehenna?

Chapter 12 -- What did we learn?

1. What could Adam and Eve have done to stay in Eden and out of the briars?
2. Gehenna is the valley of _____ and when we reject God's authority we reject God's plan for our lives?
3. The Gehenna code through-out the Bible is a word that describes living in rebellion and outside the _____ with God?
4. When Jeremiah 29:11 states God's intent, what is it that He wants for us?

5. According to Jeremiah 29:12-14 what did God say that they did or did not do?
6. What did Paul mean in 1ˢᵗ Corinthians 9:27 when he said if he did not walk carefully he would become a castaway?
7. How did this writer say that this lesson of Gehenna is a running teaching from Genesis to Revelations?
8. Put the lessons learned in this book into one sentence or a paragraph.
9. Tell me what the Gehenna Code is.
10. Write me a paragraph and explain why Gehenna is not a place that we are to live, in light of Jesus saying we are better off if we lose an eye or arm than to live in Gehenna. He thought this is that serious!

www.ingramcontent.com/pod-product-compliance
Lightning Source LLC
Chambersburg PA
CBHW030530080526
44586CB00011B/389